Bob Cousy

This is the heartwarming story of the 6 foot, 1 inch basketball ace who starred in every game he played. John Devaney takes us from the early days of the "Cooz" to that final, torturous game against the Los Angeles Lakers. We see all the things Cousy could do—the incredible behind-the-back dribbling and those blind passes, the fantastic hook shots and those lone one-handed bombs from 25 to 30 feet away. Bob Cousy learned the technique of surprise from his first coach, Morty Arkin, and out of those training sessions would come all the fabulous moves and tricks that the basketball world recognized with his nickname, the Houdini of the Hardwood.

BOB COUSY

By John Devaney

G. P. Putnam's Sons • New York

TO DELIA DEVANEY

Third Impression

© 1965 by John Devaney
All Rights Reserved
Published simultaneously in the Dominion of
Canada by Longmans Canada Limited, Toronto
Library of Congress Catalog Card Number: 65-10866
MANUFACTURED IN THE UNITED STATES OF AMERICA
10216

CONTENTS

1	Last Time for the Cooz	9
2	"We Win the Big Ones, Huh?"	17
3	They Called Him "Flenchy"	33
4	"We Ought to Play Basketball!"	45
5	Best in the City	58
6	A Man Called Doggie	70
7	Good-bye to Girls and Holy Cross	82
8	"Cousy's a Bum"	96
9	"A Winner At Last"	110
10	At Home with Cousy	125
11	"You Get Used to It"	136
12	The Champs No Longer	147
13	"Better Be Your Best, Bob"	158
14	A Prayer for a Last Favor	172
15	Joe Dillon Said It Best	179
	Bob Cousy's All-Time Records	188
	Index	190

ACKNOWLEDGMENT

THE MATERIAL for this book was drawn from many sources, since much has been written about Bob Cousy over the years. But the author would like in particular to express his thanks to Al Hirshberg, co-author with Cousy of *Basketball Is My Life,* and to Steve Gelman, author of *Bob Cousy, Magician of Pro Basketball.* Their books proved especially valuable, and are highly recommended to those who would like to learn more about the Cooz.

The author also owes a debt to these writers who have written magazine and newspaper articles on Cousy: Irv Goodman, Ed Linn, Dave Anderson, Robert Rice, Herbert Warren Wind, John Underwood, William Leggett, and Phil Elderkin.

BOB COUSY

CHAPTER 1

Last Time for the Cooz

HE CAME pounding down the hardwood floor, running in his bandy-legged way, the floppy wrists dribbling the ball low to the ground, controlling it as surely as if it were a yo-yo on a string. The long, dark face was expressionless as he looked first one way, then the other. He crossed the midcourt line, cut, and then—like a man hit by a bullet—he went down.

The big crowd, 15,000 jammed into the Los Angeles Sports Arena, let out a loud Oooooh! On the floor, Bob Cousy writhed, clutching his left ankle, his face twisted in pain.

Out from the Boston Celtic bench ran coach Red Auerbach and trainer Buddy LeRoux.

"What happened?" asked Auerbach.

"I tripped," said Cousy. "The ankle—it hurts. I think maybe it's sprained."

Carefully, leaning on LeRoux's shoulder, Cousy

stood up. He winced as he put pressure on the left foot. "C'mon," said LeRoux, "let's get to the dressing room. I'll put some ice on that foot."

Disgust on his face, Cousy looked up at the big square scoreboard high above the court. "Ten minutes too soon," he said to LeRoux, "ten minutes too soon."

In chalk-white electric lights, the scoreboard showed a little more than ten minutes left in the game. Another pattern of bulbs showed the score: Boston 92, Los Angeles 83. This was the sixth game of the best-of-seven series for the 1962-1963 National Basketball Association championship. Boston was leading, three games to two. If the Celtics could hold this lead for another ten minutes, this team of Cousy and big Bill Russell and Frank Ramsey, of Tommy Heinsohn and the Jones boys, K. C. and Sam, of Satch Sanders and rookie John Havlicek—this team would erase all doubts that it was the greatest ever by bringing back to Boston the Celtics' fifth straight world championship.

Five straight championships. Three words. A cliché of the sports pages: five straight, ten straight, twenty straight. We toss off the phrases lightly. But consider this about five straight championships: Only two teams—baseball's Yankees and hockey's Canadians—had ever before won five straight championships in any major sport. No one else—not the Giants nor Dodgers in baseball, not Green Bay nor the Giants nor Notre Dame nor Oklahoma in football.

A year earlier, the Celtics had won their fourth championship, barely beating the Los Angeles Lakers in the waning moments of the final game. "Lucky Celtics," howled the Los Angeles fans, and now—in the Sports Arena—there were huge placards pleading Go LAKERS, SMASH THE SMELTICS.

But behind the placards, anxious eyes now looked down on Cousy's twisted figure. "Cousy's hurt," the Laker fans yelled. "He's going out of the game. The old guy's finished. Let's go, Lakers!"

On the floor, the Lakers—led by the rangy Jerry West and the sleek and graceful Elgin Baylor—wiped their faces with towels. They watched Cousy being helped off the floor. This is a team of pros; if they felt pity for Cousy, their faces did not show it.

But it was a time for pity. And even this fanatical crowd sensed it as Cousy, a green jacket bunched over his shoulders, limped toward a doorway marked EXIT. This was the exit for the great Bob Cousy—the Cooz, they had called him. A few weeks earlier he had announced that he would retire at the end of the play-offs after 13 years as a star in the National Basketball Association. But this was no exit in glory, leaving with a limp, the victory far from won. As he had said, he was leaving ten minutes too soon.

The game resumed and the crowd burst into a roar as Baylor drove in to score on a hook. Now the Boston lead was down to seven. Jerry West threw in a jumper and the Los Angeles fans were on their feet, yelling for baskets. In a seat near courtside, TV's Danny Thomas nervously rammed a cigar in and out of his mouth. A few feet away, Doris Day bobbed up and down, and singer Pat Boone nervously blew bubbles of gum.

Down in the dressing room, a cavernous concrete-walled room, you could hear the muffled roaring of the crowd. Cousy watched fretfully as LeRoux put ice bags on the ankle. "I fell over my own foot," he said to LeRoux. "I must be getting old. How stupid can you get?"

Someone opened the door and it was like a radio suddenly turned on high. "Baylor just scored," a man yelled over the din. "They're only four behind."

Cousy grimaced. If the Lakers won, he knew he would not be able to play in the seventh game. The ankle would be tight for a week.

Cousy glared down at the hot, puffing ankle. "Buddy," he said, "tape the blinking thing up quick."

Out on the court you could see that something was gone from the Celtics. Big Bill Russell was corkscrewing his 6-11 frame high into the air to snare rebounds, then turning and firing the ball upcourt to one of the Celtics' guards. It was the pass—the "outlet" pass—that had begun so many devastating Celtic fast breaks. But the Celtic machinery, like an automobile engine with wet spark plugs, sputtered, and the Celtics moved slowly and laboriously. They were five men suddenly awkward in each other's presence, moving without precision or timing, running into each other on switches, arriving a half-step too late on screens.

The Lakers were scoring two baskets for every one by the Celtics. Now—with 4:20 left in the game—that big nine-point lead had shrunk to one, 100-99.

Auerbach leaped off the bench, his hands forming a T as he signaled to the Celtics to call time out. The referee's whistle shrieked. Play stopped. Slowly the players walked toward their benches.

And then the crowd let out a sudden, unexpected shout. The Cooz was coming out through the archway under the EXIT sign, limping on the taped-up ankle. The players turned and looked at him, the faces of the Lakers impassive, the faces of the Celtics wearing big grins. The Cooz was back.

He limped to the bench, threw off the Kelly-green jacket, and joined the clump of Celtics around Auerbach. No one asked whether he would play. It was just understood: Cousy was back, and he had come back to play.

The Celtics had the ball and suddenly they were exploding downcourt again. Someone cut, Cousy threw a pass. Two points!

But Baylor came back to score for Los Angeles and the Boston lead was still only one point, 102-101. Slowly Cousy dribbled the ball downcourt, limping perceptibly on that bad ankle. He was no longer a threat to drive past his man, but now he would prove again what he had once said a long time ago: "I can be important to this team without scoring a point." He was the Celtics' captain, the bandmaster, the puppeteer pulling the strings. He threw another quick pass to Heinsohn, who was fouled. The big, muscled Heinsohn sank two foul shots and the Celtics were ahead, 104-101.

Moments later it was 104-102. The time on the big electric scoreboard read 2:50, then 2:49, then 2:48 as the Lakers brought the ball upcourt. Jerry West arched a pass to burly Rudy LaRusso. But the pass was a little too high, a little too soft. Boston's Tommy Heinsohn darted in front of LaRusso, snatched the ball, stumbled once, regained his balance, and dribbled half the length of the court to sink the lay-up. The Celtics led, 106-102.

Still the Lakers weren't quitting. They scored to trail again by two, and everyone in the arena was standing, yelling and screaming. But Cousy's face was impassive, a man on his way to a funeral, as he brought the Celtics downcourt. Boston scored again, but with 45 seconds to go, the Lakers' Dick Barnett spun through the air, tossing a spectacular reverse-spin shot that went in.

The whistle sounded. Barnett had been fouled. He walked to the line, took a deep breath, aimed in the sudden silence, and sank the shot.

A thunderclap of noise shook the arena. Danny Thomas and Doris Day jumped up and down, clapping and yelling hoarsely. The Lakers trailed by only a point, 108-107. There were 43 seconds left.

Cousy moved the ball across midcourt. His eyes looked up quickly at the scoreboard as the big white lights flashed off the seconds. By NBA rules, the Celtics had to shoot within 24 seconds or lose the ball. Cousy cut, feinted, dribbled, using up most of that 24 seconds. Then he shot, a quick and soft jumper.

The ball hit the rim, bounced off into a tangle of straining arms and hands. A Laker grabbed the ball, lost it, and now Tommy Heinsohn was chasing after it, desperation on his face. He snapped up the ball, wheeled to shoot, and was fouled. Heinsohn sank the two foul shots and Boston led, 112-107.

The dogged Lakers swarmed upcourt and scored to trail, 112-109. But now there were less than 24 seconds left; if the Celtics could hold the ball, they would win. And as he had done so often in the past 13 years, Auerbach was up off the bench and signaling to the Celtics: Give the ball to the Cooz.

Cousy brought the ball across midcourt, dribbling quickly, each bounce of the ball ticking off precious split seconds. The Lakers had to have that ball, and now one charged low at Cousy, arms flailing, but the Cooz slithered away, the ball still bouncing tantalizingly in front of him. Another Laker cut in on his blind side; Cousy wheeled, still dribbling, and darted clear.

Then suddenly, ripsawing through that din like a foghorn, came the sound of the buzzer. In center court Cousy wheeled and threw the ball high. He jumped into big Bill Russell's arms; then out came Auerbach, and he and Cousy—these two who had been together through so much for these past 13 years—were hugging each other in triumph.

Somehow they got off court, NBA champions for an unprecedented fifth time. In the dressing room, Cousy sat on the trainer's table, delicately fingering the taped ankle, the sweat standing out in huge beads on his face.

"I guess it was a little bit of old age creeping up on me," Cousy was telling the reporters who had gathered around him. "I never sprained an ankle in thirteen years."

Across the room Bill Russell was talking about Cousy. "It meant a lot for Bob," he said, "finishing his career with a winner. I tell you, for him to have closed out his career on anything less than a winner, it would have been a crime."

Later a reporter asked Cousy about something he had noticed. When the final buzzer sounded, Cousy's lips had been moving. What had he said?

He had said a prayer of thanksgiving, said Cousy. "God granted me my last wish as an athlete. We're going off as champions. A man couldn't ask for more. A man couldn't ask for anything more."

CHAPTER 2

"We Win the Big Ones, Huh?"

IF YOU got to know him well, you remember the Cooz in a thousand ways. He has a long, dark, pointed face, a hungry kind of face. Usually it's empty of any expression, solemn and calm, and if you should meet Cousy walking down a street in Worcester, Mass., where he lives, you might think he was in some kind of trance. He nearly always wears a preoccupied look, a man listening to distant music. But when he sees you, he'll stop and shake your hand, and say (if your name is Frank), "Hello, Frank, how are you today?"

He'll mention your name often when he talks to you, and if you are at all human, you'll be flattered. And you'll go away saying what a decent, nice person Bob Cousy is.

And you'll be one of thousands.

Bob is 6-foot-1, but he seems shorter, perhaps because you saw him so often playing in the NBA where they run to seven foot and higher. He has wide, sloping shoulders, and long arms that reach almost to his knees. Thus he can extend his arm out farther from his body for a sweeping hook shot than some men three or four inches taller. His hands are gigantic, so big that he can grab a basketball as though it were a grapefruit and sling it the full length of a basketball court (most baseball scouts are convinced that Cousy would have become a great shortstop).

His calm, easygoing, almost lethargic manner—off the basketball court—comes from his father. "My father is so calm," he once said, "that if our house had caught fire, he probably wouldn't have said a word."

But on the court, while the face remains calm and impassive, he is a man pursued by demons. As he must be, for basketball is a game of controlled fury. "This is a game," he once told writer Herbert Warren Wind, "where you've got to put out your top effort every second. You're head to head with your man. In the final analysis, it's how much better you can sustain your drive, your purpose, than he can. That's what makes a man, and a team, superior."

You listen and you remember how often he was the man superior, off the court and on it.

Like the night in 1949 when he was playing for Holy Cross against Loyola. . . .

The score was tied, 57-57, with 15 seconds left and the Boston Garden a bedlam. Cousy had the ball at midcourt. He dribbled toward the foul line, with Loyola's Gerry Nagel guarding him tightly on the right side. Cousy reached the foul line, but now Nagel was all over him on the right side, blocking the obvious route to the basket. Suddenly Cousy stopped short, swung the ball behind his back, bounced it into his left hand, then cut toward the basket from the left side.

Dumbfounded, Nagel was left standing at the foul line. Another Loyola player swung over to guard Cousy, but Bob spun and threw a hook shot with his left hand. The ball caromed off the backboard and into the basket.

Loyola came back with a foul shot, but seconds later the game was over, Holy Cross winning, 59-58. Later, Cousy told Holy Cross sports editor Dave Anderson: "When I saw Nagel all over me on the right side, it was the only thing I could do. I didn't think about it. I just did it."

Did Cousy mean that he had never practiced the behind-the-back dribble before?

"No," he said. "I've practiced the left-hand hook shot many times, of course, but never the behind-the-back dribble."

In the Loyola dressing room, Nagel shook his head. "I had him covered," he said, "and then he sort of disappeared. The guy is a magician."

It was the spring of 1963. A few weeks before, halfback Paul Hornung had been banned from National Football League games for a year for betting. Hornung had always been a lively one, the kind everybody liked, but right after his suspension was announced, the phone in his Louisville home didn't ring very often. Lots of people don't like to run with losers.

But one morning the phone did ring. It was Bob Cousy calling from San Francisco, where the Celtics were playing that night. Cousy and Hornung had been friends for years.

"Paul," said Cousy, "they're having a testimonial dinner for me in Worcester early in April. I want you to be there."

And at that dinner, Hornung was placed next to Cousy at the table for the guests of honor. When Hornung got up to make his first public appearance since the suspension, Cousy rose, and then all of Cousy's friends rose, and they gave Hornung a five-minute standing ovation. Finally, Hornung—his voice catching—began to speak.

"One of the first people to call me last week," he said, "was Bob Cousy. And Bob said, Paul, I want you to be here. I'll never forget it."

You remember all the things he could do: the incredible behind-the-back dribbling and those blind passes that he would whip to a man all alone under the basket; how he led those Celtic fast breaks that swept like summer rainstorms from one end of the court to the other; the fantastic hook shots off his ear and those long one-handed bombs from 25 or 30 feet away; and how he could dribble and dribble and dribble while five men fell on their pants trying to take it away from him.

"Someday," said a referee once, "somebody's going to tell me that Cousy has just swallowed the ball, and

I'm simply going to go over to the bench to get a new one."

When Bill Russell first came to the Celtics, he seemed to resent Cousy's publicity. "I've never been fooled by a Cousy pass," he said. "I played with K. C. Jones in college, and K. C. is trickier than Cousy."

Someone else who thought K. C. trickier was Charles Harney, a West Coast contractor. He had watched K. C. dribble and pass spectacularly for the University of San Francisco before going on to play with the Celtics. Once Harney told Walter Brown, a co-owner of the Celtics, "Nobody could be more spectacular than K. C."

Then, for the first time, Harney saw Cousy play. After the game, Harney sat down and wrote to Brown: "I saw Cousy last night and I know what you mean. I still think K. C. is great, but it's like comparing a boy to his father."

The Celtics were playing an exhibition game in Raleigh, North Carolina, early in 1951. On the team was Chuck Cooper, the first Negro to play in the NBA. When the Celtics checked into their hotel, they were told that Cooper would have to stay at another hotel. Cooper went to the hotel. It was dirty and infested with bugs. Disgusted, Cooper decided to catch a late train out of Raleigh after the game rather than stay over until the next morning, when the Celtics were flying back to Boston.

Cousy heard what Cooper was going to do. He went

to Auerbach. "I think I'll go back on the train with Cooper," he said.

"Go ahead," said Auerbach, barely hiding his surprise. The train was a dusty rattler that wouldn't be leaving Raleigh until three in the morning.

After the game, the tired Cousy and Cooper trudged around the streets of Raleigh. Drugstore cowboys threw hard looks at Cousy, walking alongside the tall Negro, but nobody said anything. Bob and Chuck decided to buy a couple of cans of beer to while away some time, but at the package store, Cooper and Cousy saw that there were two entrances, one labeled WHITE, the other COLORED.

They walked away without saying a word.

At 3 A.M. they boarded the train together for a long, jouncing ride northward. Later, people complimented Cousy on what he had done. "Why?" he said, honest surprise in his eyes. "Why? We were teammates, weren't we?"

Red Auerbach was delighted with his new red fedora. He held it with tender, loving care; rarely did he let it out of his sight. Even when he took a shower after practice, he'd put the hat on a nearby chair so he could look at it.

But one afternoon, as he peeked out of the shower to look at that wonderful hat, he saw that it was gone. Horror on his face, he leaped out of the shower, dripping, and yelled: "Where's my hat? Who took my hat?"

"Don't get excited, Red," said Cousy. "I know exactly where your hat is."

"I'll murder somebody if anything happens to that hat," said Auerbach. "Where is it?"

"Right there," said Cousy.

He jerked a thumb at one of the other showers. Big Easy Ed Macauley was standing under a torrent of water, wearing Auerbach's beloved fedora. Shouting an oath to kill, Auerbach leaped into the shower, but Macauley tossed the fedora to Cousy, who airily began to cut it up with scissors.

His face red, roaring threats, Auerbach stomped out of the room. He threw on his clothes and walked angrily to his car. On the seat he found a brand-new red fedora, identical to the one he had owned, and with it a card that read, *From the boys.*

Someone walked into the Celtic dressing room and asked Cousy about his thigh, which he had injured several weeks earlier. "I thought you were going to need an operation on it," the visitor said.

"Heck, it wasn't going to be any operation," Cousy said. "Just a needle to do some draining."

But one of the Celtics overheard and said: "Yeah, that's why he was taking tranquillizers for two weeks."

It was beginning to snow outside and the temperature was around ten degrees. In the small unheated room under the Boston Garden, a photographer and this writer shivered in our heavy overcoats. From above, reverberating off the bare concrete walls, we could hear the sounds of the crowd, waiting expectantly for the start of the 1957 NBA All-Star game.

The photographer, Ben Ross, and I were at the Garden to take color photos of five NBA stars for the cover of a magazine. We had photographed Bob Pettit, Dolph Schayes, George Yardley and Neil Johnston. Cousy was the last name on our list, but now there was only 15 minutes before the start of this important game.

Cousy came into the room noiselessly. As usual before a game, he was quiet, a melancholy frown on his face. Slowly he pulled off the warm-up suit. Watching him as he stood there in his basketball shorts and shirt, I shivered inside my heavy coat.

"OK," said Ross, "I'm ready to shoot." Cousy dribbled a ball toward the camera, but there was no flash from the array of special lights around the room.

"Hell," said Ross, "something's gone wrong with the strobe lights."

A flush of embarrassment swept my face. "I'm sorry, Bob," I said. "Would you mind waiting, just a minute?"

He said nothing, staring vacantly at the walls in that trancelike way he has. Five minutes crept by as Ross fiddled with the lighting. Goose pimples were sprouting in angry red patches on Cousy's bare arms and legs. Finally he turned and said, "I'm sorry, but I'll have to go now."

He tugged on the warm-up suit. Just as Cousy had

finished with the last of a half-dozen zippers, Ross yelled: "Wait a minute. I got them working now."

"Never mind, Bob," I said. "You'd better get out onto the floor or you'll miss a chance to warm up."

He didn't say a word, but he bent down and began unzippering the suit, the face still expressionless. He shed the pants, turned to Ross, and said: "I'm ready."

The pictures were taken. By the time Cousy got back upstairs, he had less than three minutes to warm up for this prestige-filled game.

He came into the game midway through the first period with the West leading, 18-14. He was the spearhead of a series of sudden fast breaks that rang up 11 straight points for the East. The burst flustered the West team, which missed five straight free throws. At the half, though, the West still led by a point.

Early in the third period, Cousy fired a succession of quick passes into big Neil Johnston, who scored 15 points with sweeping hook shots during the next five minutes, and the game was in the bag for the East.

Minutes after it had ended, Bob Cousy was called out to stand in the spotlight at center court. There he was awarded a trophy as the game's Most Valuable Player.

Cousy once talked about how he keyed himself up for a game. "Like suppose we are playing the Lakers," he said. "I think about Dick Barnett, the man I'll be playing head to head, and how he scored twenty-five or thirty points against me the last time we played. I think about how he made me look bad on plays. I build myself up into a state—well, if Barnett were to walk into my room a few hours before the game, I might try to stuff a basketball down his throat."

The chauffeur-driven limousine sped toward Boston on a frigid January afternoon in 1949. Inside the car were three Holy Cross players—Cousy, Dermie O'Connell, and Joe Mullaney—on their way to the Garden for a big game against Loyola. O'Connell and Mullaney were singing a current song hit, "On a Slow Boat to China." When they finished, Mullaney looked at Cousy, who was staring moodily out the window.

"Give us a song, Cooz," said Mullaney.

"What for?" said Cousy, still looking out the window. "Like they say, it's a game of think."

It had been a typical first half for the Cooz. He had taken only six shots, sinking three of them and making a foul shot, for a total of seven points. But in the second half, he began to drive. He hit on a hook, then threw in two long one-handers, and drove around his man for another hook. You could see his opponent, who had played him so tightly and fiercely during the first half, visibly giving up.

"They come out during the first half all fired up," he once said. "So in the first half I take only the shots I know I'm going to make. Then you start to look for signs that the other guy is getting weary—mentally or physically.

"There are ways you can tell. When he begins to go

behind a pick instead of fighting his way through or when he begins to lag back a little.

"What I have going for me is human nature."

He played each game with the fiery spirit of a man who thought that this game might be his last. On the eve of his retirement, some of his friends held a two-day tribute to him in Worcester. As part of the affair, a game was arranged between a pro team captained by Cousy and a team of college all-stars. A reporter watched Cousy running up and down the court, throwing his right arm up high whenever he scored a basket. "Look at him," said the reporter. "You'd think he was playing against the Lakers for the championship."

Later one of his Holy Cross teammates, Andy Laska, was talking about how hard Cousy played. "You'd be playing against him in a little pickup game at his summer camp and you'd take the ball away from him. He'd knock you into the woods to get it back."

Cousy was going to be the goat of the game. Everybody knew it, and lots of people were happy. When you've been on top for a long time, there are those who are glad to see you take a tumble. "It's about time he got his," they'll say.

Now Cousy—playing in the 1954 All-Star game before a packed house at New York's Madison Square Garden—was about to get his. The East had been leading by two points with only a few seconds remaining. Cousy had the ball near center court, dribbling out the clock, when the West's Bob Davies swooped in, stole the ball, and dribbled the length of the court to score the tying basket.

Cousy was going to be the goat all right, and they smiled thinking about it as they watched him dribble the ball downcourt, his face showing no concern. The seconds were ticking off: ten, nine, eight, seven . . .

Suddenly Cousy cut toward the foul circle, spun, and threw a quick hook shot off his right ear. It went in. Again the East was ahead, and though the West came back to tie the score, the East won in overtime and Cousy was voted the Most Valuable Player.

The goat was now the hero. "I make lots of mistakes," he said later. "Sometimes they cost you, sometimes they don't. The big thing is, don't get flustered by a mistake. Keep cool, keep your confidence."

The Knicks were murdering the Celtics before a cheering crowd at Madison Square Garden. Now, in the closing minutes, the Knicks' rookie, Sweetwater Clifton, was putting salt in the Celtics' wounds. A recent recruit from the Harlem Globetrotters, Clifton went into his Globetrotters' routine, twirling the ball in front of the Celtics' noses, then pulling it away, and the big crowd laughed and laughed.

And then the Cooz got mad. He grabbed a rebound, weaved through the Knickerbockers until suddenly he was face to face with Clifton. Cousy made a big windmill motion with his right arm, as if to throw his famous long pass. Clifton leaped high into the air to block it.

There was no pass.

As Clifton came down to the ground, a foolish look on his face, he saw what Cousy had done with the ball: letting it slide down his arm, across the nape of his neck, then down his back. Cousy caught the ball with his left hand, then stuck out his empty right hand to "shake" with Clifton.

The crowd roared; this was an old Globetrotter trick. Clifton grinned, but it was the weakest grin seen in a long time at Madison Square Garden.

A few weeks later a reporter asked Cousy how long he'd been practicing the trick. "I'll tell you the truth," he said. "I'd been practicing it for a while, but it was very seldom I could get it to work."

Suppose it hadn't worked in front of the huge, jeering New York crowd?

"I guess," said Cousy, smiling, "I would have looked pretty stupid."

Instead, said a reporter, he had made Clifton look pretty stupid.

"I know," he said. "And afterward I was sorry I had done it. I didn't mean to make a rookie like Clifton look bad. The next time I was in New York, I called him up and told him I was sorry."

There had been a bad fire in Worcester, and two firemen were killed putting out the blaze. A day later Bob Cousy was on the phone, calling up Carl Braun of the Knicks and some other pro stars. A few weeks later, Cousy and his friends put on a basketball game before a big crowd in Worcester. All the money went to the families of the two firemen.

It was April, 1959, and the Celtics were playing the Syracuse Nationals in the play-offs for the Eastern title. It was a best-of-seven series; the two teams were tied, three games apiece; this, the final game, was being played before a capacity throng at the Boston Garden.

Syracuse, led by the great Dolph Schayes, was hot. At the half the Nats led by 17 points. As the Celtics slowly walked to their dressing room, the boos rolled out of the balconies. "You're choking up, ya bums," they yelled, remembering how often in the past Syracuse had knocked Boston out of play-offs.

As the second half began, Cousy pulled the Celtics around him. "If we're going to lose," he said, "I might as well be the goat. I'm going to start calling my plays. Get me the ball."

The Celtics got the ball to Cousy and the ball started going in. Boston closed the gap, then moved into a slight lead, but Schayes went on a spree and with two minutes to go, Syracuse led by seven.

Cousy called time out. He slumped to the floor, exhausted, the sweat plastering the green shirt to his skinny body. "Feed me," he said. "Get me that ball."

He drove for a lay-up. Two points. He drove again. Another two points. First Russell fouled out, then Heinsohn.

Still Cousy kept running, the breath coming now in great unnatural heaves, the lungs on fire. "I thought they would just explode," he said later, "and that would be the end of it."

He took a pass near the key and dropped in a one-hander. He turned to run back upcourt, then suddenly wheeled, intercepted a Syracuse pass and scored on a lay-up.

The score was tied.

Syracuse called time out. Cousy sank to his knees.

Buddy LeRoux came out and put an ice pack on his neck. And from the tiered seats, the thousands looked down, subdued and whispering now, no longer throwing taunts of "choke" and rolling out boos. Someone hollered—and you could hear it clearly above the hush—"Cooz, get up, Cooz!"

He did get up. He stole a pass from Larry Costello, threw it to Ramsey, who missed the shot, but Cousy barged into the mass of bodies under the basket and tapped in the rebound. He drove, scored and was fouled on a shot. He sank the free throw for a three-pointer and now the Celtics led, 130-125.

He ran back to cover his man, legs wobbling, gagging as he tried to get his breath, his eyes glazed with exhaustion. There were only 23 seconds left when the Celtics got the ball again—still ahead by five—and Auerbach was up from the bench, flashing the familiar signal: Give the ball to Cooz.

He had it in center court and he was dribbling out the clock. The Nats had to have that ball, and first one, then two and even three men began to harry him, swarming all over him, but Cousy ducked and feinted, somehow avoiding being fouled and somehow keeping that bouncing ball in front of him.

The huge crowd was on its feet, counting off the seconds—*three, two, one*—and then the buzzer sounded and a happy roar swelled over the Garden. The Celtics surrounded Cousy, grabbed him, kissed him, pulled him, carried him toward the dressing room. And suddenly all the strength was gone; he was a trembling, limp rag doll and they had to hold him by the arms and carry him into the dressing room.

There he lay on a table for 45 minutes, too exhausted even to speak. The Celtics, one by one, came by him, grabbing his arm, ruffling his hair, patting his back, the obeisances of pros to a super-pro. Finally, the breath still coming between the words in tortured heaves, he turned to a newspaperman and said, "Well, we showed 'em, huh? We showed 'em we don't choke up. We showed 'em we win the big ones, huh?"

To a pro, there is no sin greater than choking up, collapsing under pressure. The ballplayers call it "taking the apple." You look back at the life of Bob Cousy and you see a guy who made mistakes—in basketball and away from basketball. He is a human being, and so he is not perfect. But in a lifetime in which he was tempted far more times than most of us, Bob Cousy never took the apple.

CHAPTER 3

They Called Him "Flenchy"

THE block ran almost to the edge of the East River. It was a block like many blocks on New York's East Side in the thirties. On one side were the apartment houses of the rich, towering majestically above the river. On the other side, hunched in the shadows of the larger buildings, were the five- and six-story walk-ups of the poor.

The Cousys lived on the wrong side of the block. In fact, for a long while they lived in the worst tenement in the block. Finally it was condemned as unlivable and they moved to another walk-up, one that was only a little better.

Sitting in front of the walk-up one hot summer afternoon, little Bob Cousy watched a rich boy come out of the building across the way; the rich boy was holding the hand of his governess.

"Sissy!" yelled one of Cousy's pals.

"Go jump in the river," hollered back the rich boy.

Cousy's pal spit into the street. "Let go of that lady watchdog," he shouted, "and I'll put *you* into the river."

Suddenly the rich boy broke loose from his governness and charged across the street. The slum kid met him halfway, and the two pitched into each other with a flurry of punches.

It was no contest. The rich boy was pulled off by his near-hysterical governess, his nose pouring blood. The poor boy was surrounded by his admiring friends.

Recalling the incident later in his autobiography *Basketball Is My Life,* written with Al Hirshberg, Cousy said:

> For months afterward, the kid from our side of the street was my hero. I always figured he'd have beaten the rich boy's brains out if the governess had let him.
>
> The moral? Well, I happen to think that there's quite a point there. So much so that I've been willing to bet on a hungry kid over a well-fed kid ever since. But don't think that I don't admire the rich kid for having broken away from his protector. It's just that you're more likely to win when you have to fight to live.

Robert Joseph Cousy—his mother called him "Roby"—was born on August 9, 1928, on East 83rd Street near East End Avenue. His mother and father, Joseph and Juliet Cousy, had come to America only a few months before, eager to make their fortune.

What they soon found instead was a nation gripped by the gray despair of a depression. Haggard men sold apples at street corners; long lines of the hungry waited outside soup kitchens for food; and everywhere there were the signs No Jobs Today.

Joseph Cousy had been a farmer back in France, but he had also driven taxicabs. Finally, after weeks of making the rounds of employment offices, he became one of the lucky ones: he got a job. He was hired as a taxi driver.

In those bleak days, though, not many were riding taxis. Joseph Cousy often worked 12 hours a day for seven days a week, yet what he brought home at the end of the week often did not average twenty cents an hour. The Cousys had to live where the rent was cheapest. And that meant the slums. That meant East 83rd Street.

There were cockroaches on the walls. The hallways reeked with the sour smells of a hundred decaying things. Huge cracks ran down the walls of the apartment, exposing spider webs and broken pipes. At night you could hear the rats scurrying. And always there were bugs—the bedbugs that left swelling welts on the arms and legs, the fleas that made you scratch, the roaches that crawled over the floors in brown waves.

None of this bothered little Roby Cousy. "I just assumed," he says, "that everybody in the world lived like that." His mother knew differently. Juliet Cousy had been a tall, thin, beautiful young girl. She liked nice things, and she liked her house to be immaculately clean. Night and day she scrubbed and washed, sprayed bug killers and patched up holes, but still there were the bugs. "We can't go on living like this," she told her husband day after day. "We must get out of here. We must find a place to live in the country, where Roby can breathe good fresh air."

Her husband would shrug.

Like so many husbands and wives, they were opposites. She was tall and thin; he was short and stocky. She was nervous and high-strung, the kind who worried, constantly wringing her hands over problems real or imaginary. He was calm and easygoing, never in a hurry to do anything, accepting things as they were and assuming that they would get better. If there was something to be done, Juliet Cousy fretted until it was done—the sooner the better. Joseph Cousy took the long view: It would be done when it would be done.

In both, however, there blazed an ambition to rise in the world. Though he looked upon the slums with poker-faced detachment, Joseph Cousy had set himself a goal: to get out of them as soon as possible.

Cousy inherited qualities of both his parents. On the basketball court, he had his mother's bursts of nervous energy (as well as her big frame and large hands and feet), plus his father's calmness in moments of crisis. And like his parents, he liked to set goals for himself. "For as long as I can remember," he says, "I've been setting goals, and when I reach them, I set myself some more."

Cousy grew up the same way that millions of kids grew up on the streets of New York during the thirties. His parents were "greenhorns," a name that immigrants used to kid themselves about their greenness in the new country. And like many of the German immigrants who lived in the neighborhood—it was called Yorkville—the Cousys did not speak English. Since his mother and father spoke only French to each other, Cousy did not know any other language until he was five. "I guess I was in high school," he recalls, "before I stopped thinking in French. And even now, if I have a nightmare I talk in French."

His constant use of French, plus a slight lisp, has—even to this day—impeded Cousy's ability to pronounce the letter *r*. The way Cousy pronounces it, it sounds like an *l*. For several years a speech teacher had him reciting, "Around the rugged rock the ragged rascal ran." But often it would sound like this when Cousy said it: "Alound the lugged lock, the lagged lascal lan."

Because of his ancestry, Cousy was nicknamed "Frenchy" by the kids on the block. But when they heard Cousy pronounce it, they gave him a new nickname: Flenchy.

Flenchy was a skinny, pale, birdlike kid, running the streets with the other boys and finding a hundred ways to have fun. . . .

If you were a boy living on the East Side of Manhattan during the thirties, your whole world was "The Block," the name that everyone gave to the street where they lived. Life on The Block was divided into cycles that came with mysterious suddenness. One day, for instance, all the kids took out their roller skates, clamped them on their shoes, and just like that, every kid on The Block was roller-skating. Nobody had said, "Let's all roller-skate today," yet suddenly it was roller-skating time. You skated for two or three weeks, playing hockey or tag or just skating, and then one day—again just like that—you put away your skates, took out your marbles, and now every kid on The Block was down on one knee in the gutter, spanning marbles with his fingers. Nobody had said anything, but suddenly skating was out and marble-playing was in.

Sports also came in cycles but they were tied to the seasons of the year. In the fall and winter you played "association," a game like touch football, and in the winter you played basketball in a nearby schoolyard. You played handball in the spring and fall, but the big game from early March until late in September was stickball.

Today stickball is a disappearing game, crowded off the side streets of Manhattan by the automobile. Lines of parked cars now occupy the spaces—against the curbs—that were once first base or third base on stickball diamonds.

The stickball diamond was an elongated one, with home plate usually the iron cover of a sewer in the middle of the street. First and third bases were chalked off at the curbs about 75 feet from home, with second base a chalked-out box in the center of the street, on a straight line with home plate and about 40 yards away. The pitcher's "mound" was a parenthesis-shaped chalk line about 60 feet from home.

The ball was usually one made by A. G. Spalding, pink-colored and very rubbery; it had a tremendous bounce, which was one way you could recognize what the kids called "a real Spaldeen." The bat was a broomstick with the broom sawed or burned off. There were no balls and strikes. You swung at the first pitch that appealed to you, but one miss—or two fouls—and you were out.

In most other ways, you played by baseball rules (but there was no stealing). You marked the score in chalk on a scoreboard often painted in white on the black paved street. It was a distinctively shaped scoreboard, and you saw at least one on every street on the East Side. It looked like this:

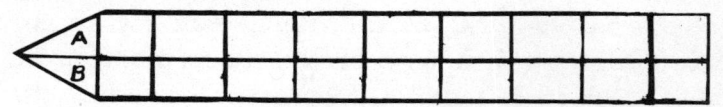

Bob Cousy played stickball the moment he got out of St. Katherine's parochial school at 3 o'clock every afternoon, all day on Saturdays (and sometimes on Sundays when his mother wasn't looking). He was one of the best stickball players on the block for his age, possessing a nimble quickness that allowed him to get in front of whizzing liners and sharply bouncing grounders. His hands were huge for such a small boy; he could grip a stickball bat with authority and he fielded wicked shots without a glove.

In fact, only a few of the kids had gloves; the big stickball problem for East Side kids was a perennial shortage of equipment. Spaldeens cost a dime, sometimes 15 cents for a really good one. Each boy would chip in a penny or two, if he had it, but before the day was out, someone would likely pull a ball too much and hit it over a roof. Unless someone knew how to get onto the building and throw the ball down, the game was ended.

Broomsticks were easier to come by, and they lasted longer—provided they weren't confiscated by the police. The cops were death on stickball, for a reason the kids could never understand: grown-ups who worried about the rubber ball somehow breaking a window.

When someone on the block called the police and the white-topped police car (the kids called it Snow White and the two dummies) swung into the street, someone would yell: "Chickee!" and then everyone scattered. One brave soul, though, would grab the stick and run with it, into his apartment house if he could get there in time, or down some stairs into the basement of an apartment house, where he could lose himself in a maze of hallways. If he were caught, though, he was likely to get a whack across the seat of his pants from one of the cops. Even worse, the cops would methodically prop every stick against the curb and then stomp them in half.

But if the cops were the natural enemy of the East Side boy, the East Side boy was the natural troublemaker for the cop. In the summer the cops were constantly being called to turn off fire hydrants; the kids turned them on to frolic in the spray. In the winter the cops were kept busy stamping out the bonfires that the kids would start in an alleyway or bank of snow.

From early spring to late summer, the cops kept a constant eye on the quick-flowing river. Like all the boys on the block, Flenchy Cousy often swam nude in the East River, flopping around among the oil slicks and orange peels, despite stern warnings from his parents that he would catch typhoid fever (and some East Side kids did catch typhoid or meningitis, dreaded words among mothers, and the boys and girls would die with shocking suddenness). Often the cops would make sudden raids on the docks along the river, and Flenchy and his friends sometimes could be seen racing toward The Block, pulling on shirts over wet bodies, the cops in hot pursuit.

One thing that Flenchy did not do—strangely enough, as his life turned out—was play basketball. Actually this was not so surprising; there were not many basketball courts on the East Side, maybe one or two in a schoolyard or playground. These were taken over by the big boys—the high school kids—from early in the morning until it got dark. For most of the little kids, the nearest they got to a basketball was standing on the sidelines and watching.

Flenchy Cousy wasn't the watching kind, and so he never even held a basketball in his hands as long as he lived on the East Side. But like all his friends, he was a collector—a collector of baseball cards, marbles, various kinds of ropes. There was even a time when Flenchy and his friends had a contest to see who had the biggest collection of the valve caps that are found on the tires of cars.

There was only one source for such a collection: cars. And Cousy and one of his friends went directly to the source. They'd walk up to a parked car, look over their shoulder to make sure that nobody was watching, then kneel down and screw off the valve. For a time they did, at any rate, until one day . . .

Cousy was busy unscrewing the valve when a heavy hand clamped down on his shoulder. "Put those back," boomed a big voice.

Cousy spun out of his crouch, his eyes widening. He was staring up at a man who looked ten feet tall to this eight-year-old boy. Cousy, his hands trembling, quickly began screwing the valves back on.

"How many more of those have you got?" the man yelled.

Terrified, Cousy admitted he had a lot.

"Where?"

"Home."

"Well, go up and bring them down."

Cousy scampered off. Too scared to hide, he returned a few minutes later with a paper bag filled with valves. The man was talking to a cop and a crowd had gathered. Up and down the block, kids were yelling, "Flenchy's in hot water," and they came running to see what would happen to him.

His face red with shame, Flenchy handed the paper bag to the man. "See?" growled the man, turning to the cop; he turned the sack upside down, dumping the collection of valves on the sidewalk.

But the crowd began to laugh, and even the cop grinned a little. At that moment, Cousy's mother appeared. She talked quietly to the cop and after a while she turned to Bob and said, "Come along, Roby."

Cousy breathed a long and happy sigh: He wasn't going to jail after all. But in telling about the incident in his autobiography, *Basketball Is My Life*, he said: "That was the end of the contest. The other kid retired with the undisputed valve-cap-collecting championship of the neighborhood."

Actually Mrs. Cousy—and the cops of the neighborhood—had little trouble with Flenchy Cousy. His grandmother, who lived with the Cousys, made sure that her grandson was faithful to his Catholic faith. "You must be sure to attend Mass every Sunday," she told him. "And at school you do what the nuns tell you." Little Flenchy listened and obeyed.

Cousy was a good student at St. Katherine's, the neighborhood parochial school, which was free to children of parents who couldn't afford the tuition. Cousy went free. When he started at the school, he could not speak a word of English, since he had spoken only French at home. At first, the other kids looked at him curiously, this pale thin-faced boy with the big hands and feet, the birdlike kid who talked a gibberish language and looked at you dumbly when you said anything to him. But within a year, Cousy had learned English well enough to speak it fluently, and he was soon one of the gang.

But watching him run the streets, his mother worried—that he might be run over by a car, that he might catch a disease in the smoky air of the city. For perhaps the ten thousandth time since they had arrived in Yorkville ten years earlier, Juliet Cousy—on a Saturday afternoon in 1938—turned to her husband and said: "Look how pale Roby is. He needs good, fresh air, country air to make him strong."

But this time Joseph Cousy did not shrug his shoulders. He had his own taxi now, and with the depression coming to an end, business had been getting better. For ten years this quiet man—as self-contained as a cat—had been saving scrupulously, denying himself many things, so that he could release his family from the slums. Now the moment for escape had come.

"Tomorrow is Sunday," he said, characteristically saving words. "We will take the taxi and drive to the country to look for a new place to live."

Juliet Cousy let out a shout of joy. Bob Cousy, playing on The Block somewhere, did not even know the decision had been made, but it was a decision that would suddenly bring him to a new world, a world filled with fresh air and sweeping fields of green grass, and a game called basketball.

CHAPTER 4

"We Ought to Play Basketball!"

THE Cousy taxicab jounced down a rutted road in St. Albans, a Long Island community on the rim of New York City. Sitting next to his father in the front seat, Roby Cousy peered out at the rolling grassy land, bare except for a small house here and there.

"Look at all that grass, *maman*," he said to his grandmother. "I didn't know there was so much grass in the whole country."

Cousy's mother laughed. "You will like the country, Roby. You will never want to live in the city again."

This trip to St. Albans was just one of many that the Cousy entourage—his father, mother and grandmother—had made to the suburbs since Joseph Cousy had decided to leave East 83rd Street. The Cousys wanted to rent a small house, one that they could afford. But they could not live too far from the center of the city, since Cousy's father had to drive his taxi there every day. On the other hand, Juliet Cousy wanted it far enough away so that her Roby could "breathe."

Now, rolling down the road in St. Albans, Mrs. Cousy looked around, sudden expectation in her dark eyes. This was what she had been looking for. St. Albans was a part of New York City, in the borough of Queens. But look at the vacant fields and breathe the fresh air. Yes, she decided, this must be where the Cousys would live.

Three weeks later the Cousys returned to St. Albans, this time to sign the final papers to rent a small house. And on one hot, sticky summer day in 1939, the Cousys lugged all their belongings down the stairs of their tenement, stuffed the bags and furniture into a borrowed pickup truck, and climbed slowly into the Cousy taxi.

Bob looked around. This would be his last few moments on East 83rd Street, the block that had been his entire world for all of his eleven years of life. He saw none of the boys he knew; he figured they were splashing around in the East River. He turned to get into the car. As he did, he noticed one boy who had gone to school with him at St. Katherine's. Cousy waved, and the boy waved back.

That's all there was. This was the impersonal and cold way of The Block, a place where you knew a lot of fellows, but if you didn't "show"—as the kids said —for a week or so, you were soon forgotten, quickly replaced by another kid who had just moved in. Cousy crawled into the taxi, somehow feeling no regret, no nostalgia as he left this hurly-burly world of black pavement and hot concrete.

The Cousy taxi followed the truck up 83rd Street, turned right on East End Avenue toward the 59th Street bridge that would take them across the East River to Queens. As the taxi turned the corner, Cousy took one last backward look at The Block.

He has never gone back. "When I left the East Side," he said later in his autobiography, "I left it and everyone in it completely."

All was confusion as the Cousys wrestled with their suitcases and furniture outside their new home in St. Albans. Mrs. Cousy shooed her Roby away as he tried to help with the suitcases. "Go off and play," she told him, fearful he might get hurt in the confusion. "But keep off the streets."

And indeed Bob quickly found that he didn't have to play in the streets any longer. Just a half-block from his home was a huge playground teeming with boys and girls. It was called O'Connell Playground, a place that Cousy would haunt for countless hours during the next seven years.

Two teams were playing baseball. This was a game that Bob had never played on East 83rd Street's hard pavement. He watched, wondering if the game were easier or more difficult than stickball.

One of the boys in the game had to leave. "What are we going to do for a shortstop?" asked one of the players.

"I play shortstop," piped up Cousy, fibbing a little.

The boys were one or two years older than he. They looked at his small frame with doubt in their eyes.

"Got a glove?" said one.

"No."

"Take mine," said one of the other boys, throwing him a glove.

Cousy trotted out to the shortstop position. Suppose he should do badly? He had never played this game before. The ball was a lot harder than a Spaldeen, and he had never tried to field a ground ball on a pebble-strewn dirt field.

Someone hit a tryout grounder at him. Cousy picked it up smoothly with those big hands and threw the ball on a line to first.

He played baseball all that day and all the next day, and then someone said, "What's your name, kid?" Suddenly he was surrounded by a flock of new friends.

In the fall Cousy started at a new school—Public School 118—which was near Farmer's Boulevard and 104th Street. The school was two miles from Cousy's home. Most of the kids made the trip by bike, but Cousy had to walk the four-mile round trip each day. Bob's father, burdened by the expenses of moving, explained that he could not buy a bike. But sometimes Bob came home footsore and occasionally he'd wonder aloud to his mother about the possibilities of getting a bike someday.

"But we can't afford it, Roby."

"I know, but I just want to remind you that I'd like one."

His father overheard. "Maybe," he said, "maybe later."

That was all Mr. Cousy said, but Bob knew his father's quiet, determined way. If his father said "maybe later," that meant he would work to get Bob the bike.

And one day in March, when he trudged wearily through the door, his mother said to him: "Look out in the backyard."

Cousy went to the window and looked. There, propped against a wall, was a glistening new bike.

"Mine?" asked Bob, his voice catching.

"Yes," said his mother, her eyes a little wet. "Yes, Roby, yours."

If you are a boy of twelve or so and you see a tree, you know what it was made for—climbing. Bob Cousy became one of the best tree climbers in St. Albans, perhaps because he was trying to make up for all the trees he had never climbed during his years on East 83rd Street. But one day, while he scrambled along a limb, he slipped and fell hard on his right arm. It was broken.

For weeks Cousy's arm was encased in a white plaster cast. One day, while Bob moped around O'Connell, unable to do much of anything because of the cast, a friend challenged him to a game of handball.

"How can I play?" asked Cousy, pointing to the arm.

"Use your left," said his friend, grinning teasingly.

"OK," said Cousy, "you're on."

His friend beat Cousy badly, since Bob could not control the direction of the ball with his left hand. But after his friend had left the playground, Cousy continued to slap the ball with his left hand against the wall, over and over again. The next day he played with his left hand again. And again he got beat.

But he was improving. For weeks, until the cast was taken off his right arm, he played handball only with his left hand, and one day he won a game. The next day he won several. And when the arm was taken out of the cast, he kept on playing with his left as well as his right hand; soon he was able to smack the ball against the wall almost as well with his left as he could with his right. "Although no one told me," wrote Cousy years later in *Basketball Is My Life,* "somehow or other I got the idea that I had something good going for myself. I made up my mind to play with both hands after my right was OK again, so I wouldn't lose the use of my left."

Unwittingly, Bob Cousy had developed a talent that would give him his first big chance in basketball.

Yet at the time, basketball—to Cousy—was only a game that the big fellows, the sixteen- and seventeen-year-old high school fellows, played at O'Connell. Sometimes Cousy would watch from the sidelines, but nobody asked him to play. He was too small.

Cousy didn't mind. His whole life was baseball. He swept up ground balls at shortstop with those big hands, like a derrick scooping sand, and he swung a bat with a flat sweep, hitting line drives that whizzed past pitchers' ears.

It was all a dream life for Cousy. One day his mother scared him when she announced, her voice ringing with Gallic pride, "Roby, we are moving—moving to our own house."

"Where?" asked Cousy, appalled that he might never see O'Connell Playground again.

But the new house that the Cousys had *bought*—no longer did they have to rent—was only a few blocks from O'Connell. Walking to the playground one day, Bob met a short, freckle-faced boy whom he had seen at O'Connell. His name was Angus Kennedy. He and Bob were the same age, twelve, and since Bob's move to a new neighborhood necessitated his transfer from his old school, PS 188, he and Angus would soon be together in the seventh grade at PS 36.

Bob and Angus talked about PS 36 for a while, and then Angus said, "You play shortstop, don't you?"

"Yeah, that's right."

"How would you like to play on my baseball team?"

"Sure. Thanks a lot."

Angus Kennedy was Bob Cousy's first real, close friend. Today they are still close friends.

In the fall of 1941, Bob entered the eighth grade at PS 36. One afternoon, standing around the schoolyard during recess, some of the boys began talking about the high school they would all be entering the following September, Andrew Jackson. "I wonder how Jackson will make out in basketball this year," someone said. Immediately there was a chorus of shrill opinions.

Cousy listened, saying nothing. Baseball was *his*

game, not basketball. But as the boys argued, he perceived that basketball and not baseball was the big game at Andrew Jackson. In fact, the school had one of the better basketball coaches on Long Island, Lew Grummond. In his quiet, intelligent way, Bob Cousy decided that if he were going to Jackson, he had better learn something about this game called basketball.

That afternoon, walking home with Angus Kennedy and Wes Field, a tall boy who was also one of Cousy's best friends (and still is), Cousy suddenly blurted out, "We ought to play basketball."

Wes Field agreed. "And hey," he said, "there's a hoop in the schoolyard at PS 36. We could shoot there."

During recess the next day, the three friends gathered under the hoop. For the first time in his life, Bob Cousy picked up a basketball and held it in those long, bony fingers. The ball felt good. He threw it upward toward the basket, his arms stiff and awkward, but this first shot by Bob Cousy ringed the hoop and went in.

His long thin face grinned. He grabbed the bouncing ball and flung it again at the hoop. He missed. He threw the ball again. He missed.

Nevertheless, as he walked home that afternoon, the glow of sinking that first shot was still warm in his stomach. "The heck with baseball," he said to Angus. "From now on I'm a basketball player."

But he was often a basketball player without a court to play on. For hours each afternoon, Cousy, Angus and Wes Field would watch the big boys playing at O'Connell. Whenever a game ended, they'd rush onto the court to take a couple of shots. But when the older boys were rested, the three "little kids" would be shooed off-court so the next game could start.

Cousy wasn't discouraged. He'd hang around on the sidelines until dusk, his hands stuffed into a jacket to keep them warm. Then, when most of the bigger boys had left and the others were too tired to play anymore, he'd go to the foul line and he'd shoot and shoot and shoot until the playground closed and he had to return the basketball to the playground office.

One afternoon, a short, heavyset man came over to him. "You're going to be a good basketball player," he said to Cousy. "But you don't know how to shoot."

Cousy stared at him.

"Would you like to learn?"

The big grin on Cousy's face said yes.

"Look me up when you come around tomorrow."

The heavyset man was Morty Arkin, the playground director at O'Connell. He became Bob Cousy's first basketball coach. The next day he showed Bob how to take a set shot, holding the ball with the fingertips instead of in the palm of the hand. He showed him how to follow through on a set shot, and how to break the wrists on a shot only at the exact moment when he released the ball.

Week after week, Cousy practiced set shots as Arkin watched, always critical but always explaining when Cousy did something wrong.

Next, Arkin showed Bob how to drive in for a lay-up. He emphasized the importance of being able to drive from the left side as well as from the right. Once, when Bob sunk a left-handed lay-up, Arkin's face showed surprise. "You've got a strong left hand," he said to Bob.

Cousy explained how he had used the left hand to play handball when he had broken his right arm.

"That was the best *break* you ever had," said Arkin, who was a much better coach than a comedian.

But later he talked to Bob about the importance of the left-handed lay-up. "It's natural for a right-hander to drive from the right," he told Bob. "But if that side is well guarded, you may have to switch and drive in from the left. If you can do that, they won't know how to play you."

Surprise. The element of surprise. Arkin kept stressing its importance in his talks with Cousy. "The big thing," he told the little black-haired boy, "is not to be stereotyped. Don't ever be predictable. The minute your opponents learn what you do, they've got you. So be sure you can do something different every time."

Cousy listened, nodding, remembering, and out of those talks with Morty Arkin would come all the fabulous moves and tricks that would cause the basketball world to dub Bob Cousy "The Houdini of the Hardwood."

Cousy practiced everything that Arkin told him, practicing whenever he could, during the winter and spring of 1941. His life was basketball, basketball and more basketball. "Roby," said his mother one day, "can't you think of anything else? You'll kill yourself with this game."

Even Angus Kennedy thought that Cousy had become a little too enthusiastic. At night, Cousy would shoot in the schoolyard at PS 36, by the light of a streetlamp that shined down on the hoop. "I'm crazy about *basketball*," Angus told Bob one icy, windswept night when Bob pleaded with him to go to the schoolyard. "But I'm not crazy."

Cousy practiced in the rain. When snow covered the court, he'd beg a shovel from the school janitor, then scrape off the snow so he could play. He'd play early in the morning. He'd play late at night.

Sometimes he even got to play a game. He, Angus, Wes Field (who was tall for his age) and a couple of other boys put together a team that played sevenbasket or ten-basket games against the older fellows at O'Connell. Cousy played with the desperation of a penniless gambler, knowing that if his team could win, he would get to play a precious fifteen or twenty more minutes on the court. But usually they would lose to the bigger and older boys, and then there would be a long hour's wait, shivering in the cold, before they got to play another game.

In the fall of 1942, Bob and Angus walked through the big front entrance of Andrew Jackson. In a month or so, Bob knew, coach Lew Grummond would issue the call for basketball tryouts. Cousy imagined how Grummond would see him shoot for the first time, that shot sharpened by all those hours of practice. And how Grummond would shout to people around him: "There is Jackson's new star."

Bob knew he couldn't fail to impress Grummond. Wasn't he the best player among all the kids at PS 36?

Hadn't he learned all about this game from Morty Arkin? Sure, he wasn't tall, 5-foot-8, but that wasn't too small for a fourteen-year-old freshman. And he was growing.

One crisp October day, Grummond announced freshman tryouts for the junior-varsity team, since it was an unwritten rule at Jackson that the freshmen did not play on the varsity. This was all right with Bob; he figured he'd play for a while on the JVs and then Grummond would move him up to the varsity.

As Bob walked confidently to the gym with Angus and Wes, he wondered what Grummond would say when he saw a youngster who had all his moves and good shots. When they got to the gym, he found more than 200 others trying out for the team, but this didn't bother Bob at all. He knew Grummond would spot him.

The coach stood in the center of the court, watching as the boys formed long lines. One by one, each boy ran in to shoot a lay-up, then ran back to the end of the line.

Now it was Bob's turn. He took a pass from a boy under the basket, dribbled in, leaped off his left foot.

Swish! A perfect lay-up.

His heart pounding, he ran back to the end of the line. He looked toward where Grummond was standing. Grummond wasn't even looking at him! How could he have missed that lay-up?

A few minutes later, Cousy drove in again for another lay-up. And that was the last shot he took. A few minutes later, Grummond blew a whistle and announced: "That's all; the names of the boys picked for the JV will be posted."

A few days later, the names were posted. After their last class, Angus, Bob and Wes raced to the gym, almost stumbling down the staircases. There was a milling crowd of boys around the bulletin board, maybe 10 or 12 deep, but Bob slipped through like an eel, and now his thin face was staring at a sheet of paper on which was typed a short list of names. The dark eyes ran up and down the list—once, twice, then a third time.

His name wasn't there. Nor was Angus'. But Wes had made the team. Obviously Grummond had been looking for the big boys. He hadn't even seen Cousy.

The crowd began to drift away. But Cousy stood there, staring, his hands shaking a little, his face drawn tight.

"It's not the end of the world," said Angus, a realist. Cousy could not even talk.

Later he went to see Morty Arkin. "Forget it," said Morty. "You'll make the varsity yet. But what you've got to do now is practice. Practice, practice, practice."

CHAPTER 5

Best in the City

BOB COUSY once told me about his childhood for an article I was writing for *Parade* Magazine. "Most every boy has a hero he idolizes," Cousy told me. "Joe DiMaggio, for instance, was the idol of most of the kids on my block when I was a kid growing up in New York City. But somehow, for reasons I don't completely understand, my idols have never been famous people. My heroes were much closer at hand. They were other kids, a year or two older, who could do things better than I could. If a fellow were a better basketball player, for instance, I would set my sights on him—first to be as good as him, then better. When I did pass him, I picked someone else, so that I always had a new and higher goal to reach.

"There was Frank Higgins, for example. He was the best basketball player in our neighborhood. When we'd choose up sides for a game in the schoolyard, he was always the first to be picked. Frank became my idol, in the sense that I wanted to be as good as he was. And as we played against each other in the schoolyard, I could see I was edging closer to him in ability."

One day he would pass Frank Higgins. But that would happen years later, before screaming crowds on a faraway basketball court in New England. . . .

All through the fall and winter of 1942 and into the spring of 1943, Cousy kept practicing, kept playing against boys like Frank Higgins on the court at O'Connell. He worked on driving from the left side. He even began experimenting with a left-handed hook shot. He hardly ever sunk it, but he'd throw it up by the hour at the PS 36 schoolyard, making a smooth arc with his left arm and flipping the ball from behind his left ear.

Other kids, lounging in the doorways to keep out of a cutting winter wind, watched him. Then, grinning, they twirled their fingers against the sides of their heads.

That Cousy kid had to be crazy. But years later, when they read about All-American Bob Cousy, they'd say, "Well, look, he had all that talent; no wonder he made it big."

They had forgotten—as people often do—about the long hours of lonely practice that Cousy had put in to polish that talent.

In the spring of 1943, Cousy began to get the chance to make the practice pay off. He and Angus formed a team, the St. Albans Lindens Juniors. They played in the Long Island Press League, which was sponsored by the local newspaper. The team played two or three evenings a week in school gyms; but to Cousy, this was only a drop of water to a man dying of thirst. He joined a parish team, St. Pascal's, which played in a Catholic Youth League on Sundays. Still not satisfied, he joined the Laureltons, a Jewish-sponsored team which played once a week.

Those were evening games. Cousy spent each afternoon of the week at O'Connell, pounding up and down the concrete court with Frank Higgins, Angus and the rest of his friends.

Summer came; school was out. To his own and his mother's surprise, Cousy had somehow managed to get a B average at school, despite all the hours he had spent on basketball. But now the books were put aside. That summer Bob was out in the glaring sunshine at O'Connell every morning and afternoon, throwing up left-handed hook shots.

There was time for other things, too. At night, he and the other fellows might race with their bicycles, or sit in the booths at a nearby drugstore, sipping malted and talking about basketball and girls and girls and basketball. There was one girl whom Cousy liked, Joan Kilduff, and on Saturdays he'd take her to a movie, and on Sundays the two of them would go with their friends to nearby Jones Beach, swimming and horseplaying in the pounding surf.

But Cousy never once forgot his No. 1 objective: making the Andrew Jackson varsity that fall. Grummond *had* to notice him.

Grummond watched as the 200 boys lined up in the gym. Each boy in turn pounded toward the basket, jumped, and sank a lay-up. Somewhere in the crowd was Bob Cousy, now a sophomore, but again Grummond did not notice him. He did jot down the names of some boys who looked promising for the JV, but Bob's name was not on his list.

This time Bob took the news jauntily. He was playing in so many games—for St. Pascal's, for the Laureltons, for the Lindens—that somehow, someday, he knew that Grummond would have to see him play.

It happened one night when Cousy was playing for the Lindens, the team he and Angus had organized, at the Andrew Jackson Community Center. As Cousy warmed up, he saw Grummond standing on the sideline. The Lindens had been running up 30 points a game and more, high scores in those days, and Grummond had decided to see how good they really were.

This was the moment that Bob Cousy had been waiting for. He had been expecting it, and so he wasn't nervous. He played loose and smooth, shooting several baskets with his left hand.

The Lindens won easily. As Cousy walked off the court, Grummond came over and blocked his way. Here's how Bob recalled their talk in his autobiography:

"Haven't I seen you over at school?" asked Grummond.

"Yes, sir."

"What's your name?"

"Bob Cousy."

"What year are you?"

"Sophomore."

"You could use a little height."

Cousy straightened himself a little.

"Are you left-handed?"

"No, sir. I'm right-handed."

"Well, you were using your left a lot out there."

"I always do."

"Well, I like a boy who can use both hands. Come to practice tomorrow. I want to see if you can make the Junior Varsity."

Cousy did make the JV. Mostly he played against the varsity in practice scrimmages, but occasionally against the JVs of other schools.

He soon learned why he had caught Grummond's eye. Grummond was a highly organized coach; his teams used only set plays. Each player had a play number; Cousy was a number-one man, meaning that in the Grummond system, he cut from the corners, shooting mostly with his left hand. Since good left-handed shooters were always scarce, Grummond kept on the prowl for lefties. Cousy, of course, wasn't left-handed, but he was the best left-handed shooter available.

Later Cousy often thought how fortunate he'd been, first in breaking his right arm, then in meeting Morty Arkin who had taught him to shoot with his left, and finally in going to a high school whose coach desperately needed a left-handed shooter.

"Suppose you weren't able to shoot with your left," an interviewer once suggested to him. "Grummond might not have picked you, you might not have played high school ball, you wouldn't have got the chance to go to college, and then you wouldn't have made it to the pros."

"I know," said Cousy, a faraway look in his eyes. "When I think about it, I shudder."

But don't call it luck. True, Cousy was the right boy at the right place when Grummond needed a left-handed shooter. But how many other talented boys would have worked hard to learn how to shoot with their left hands, as Cousy did?

Near the close of the 1943-44 season, Grummond called Cousy aside. "If you keep improving at the rate you're going," said Grummond, "I'll put you on the varsity next season."

Cousy worked that summer on polishing his feints, until he could fake and get a half-step on his man without even thinking about the move. A few days after school started in the fall of 1944, Grummond had a talk with Bob, who had now grown to 5-foot-10. Grummond made it clear that he was counting on Bob, who was only a junior, to be the leader of the team.

It was enough to turn the head of anybody, and Bob's head slowly began to pivot. His grades had been slipping; now he thought of classes only as something that you went to before basketball practice. He knew that if he flunked even one course, he couldn't play basketball, so he studied, but only hard enough to get by.

At classes he was a celebrity. The kids turned to look at him when his name was called out. Cousy didn't mind, and sometimes maybe he swaggered a bit. He fooled around a lot, the old shyness gone, and sometimes he fooled around in class, and one day he fooled around once too often.

It happened in his homeroom, where his class gathered in the mornings before going off to their various classes in English, history, and so on. In the homeroom, the teacher took attendance, but she also gave a course in "citizenship." It was a snap course, and nobody ever studied for it, least of all Cousy.

Cousy spent most of his time at citizenship class whispering jokes to a fellow comedian who sat near him. "Stop that," the teacher warned them. "You two are not paying attention."

They'd stop for a while, and then they'd start in again. The teacher would give them another warning, but Cousy paid her little mind.

The midterm marks came out in November. Confidently, Cousy looked at his report card, and suddenly his face went pale. He looked again. No, it was still there: the big "F" next to CITIZENSHIP. He got up from his desk, watery-kneed, and almost stumbled toward the teacher's desk.

"You gave me a flunking mark in citizenship," he said. "Now I can't play basketball."

"I warned you," said the teacher.

"Yes, but I can't play basketball." Tears welled. "Please, I won't talk to anyone in class again."

"You should have thought of that before."

"You don't know what you're doing to me. Now I can't play basketball. Why won't you let me play?"

"You can play basketball or talk in class. You can't do both."

Cousy walked out of the room, gulping hard. He had worked so hard to make the team—and now he had muffed his big chance.

He had a sudden thought: Lew Grummond would fix everything. Hadn't Lew said that he was counting on Cousy? Grummond would use his influence to get the teacher to change her grade. Cousy almost ran to the gym.

"My homeroom teacher," he blurted out at the surprised Grummond, "she flunked me in citizenship. Now I can't play basketball. Can't you do anything?"

"Why did she flunk you?"

Bob's voice was tight and he was near tears, but somehow he got out the words: "For talking in class."

"Were you talking?" Grummond asked, looking Cousy right in the eyes.

"Yes. A little."

"Did she warn you?"

"A couple of times, I guess."

Now Grummond was looking harder at Cousy. "Is that all?"

"Well, maybe it was a half-dozen or so."

Grummond was silent for about a minute. "Bob," he said, finally, "I need you on this team."

Cousy's face lit up.

"But I'm not going to ask that teacher to change your mark."

Cousy looked at him, his eyes unbelieving. Grummond held up his hand. "If she hadn't warned you," he said, "maybe I'd try to do something. But she evidently told you repeatedly to stop, and you didn't stop. She had a right to flunk you. If it had been me, I would have done the same thing."

"But what about my basketball?"

"You can work out with the team. But you can't play until the next marks come out."

"That won't be until February." Then the season would be half over, and to Cousy, losing a half season of varsity basketball was like losing fifty thousand dollars.

"I know it," Grummond said. "And maybe between now and then you'll learn to keep your mouth shut in the classroom. In the meantime, you can use your spare time most wisely by studying."

That night Cousy stewed, imagining how one day he would get back at his homeroom teacher for being so mean. And Grummond, too. Why were they down on him? Well, he'd show them. He'd . . .

And on and on he raged at the world. It would be years later, when he was older and could see things with a more mature perspective, that he came to realize who was really at fault—Bob Cousy.

When he had cooled down, Cousy decided to take Grummond's advice and study. He jacked up his grades from the 70's to the 80's, a pickup that would be of great help to him just a year later.

In late January, Cousy got his next report card. On it there was a big A for citizenship.

The team had been doing well without Cousy; in fact, it was leading the Queens division of the Public School Athletic League. The night after Cousy showed Grummond his report card with the big A, Jackson played Bryant High School. Cousy started for Jackson.

He was a bundle of pent-up fury. On the opening tap, he grabbed the ball, raced all alone to the basket and scored. He scored again. He threw in a hook. He drove for a lay-up, then threw in a long two-handed set shot. He was running wild, doing things that weren't in the carefully planned Grummond book of plays. But Grummond understood; he let Cousy blow off all that energy that had been building within him. Jackson won easily, with Cousy scoring 28 points.

It was like a high school boy scoring 50 today. The next day all the New York papers had headlines:

COUSY SCORES 28 FOR JACKSON

Bob read each headline eagerly, over and over again. His mother clipped out the stories and put them in a scrapbook, one that would grow and grow, for the headlines kept on coming. A week after the Bryant game, Cousy played in Madison Square Garden. He looked up at the rising tiers of seats and imagined thousands cheering as he threw in one shot after another.

The thousands would cheer later on, but on this afternoon there were only a few hundred high school students in the Garden. However, they cheered Cousy as he scored more than 20 again and Jackson won the game.

Jackson went on to win the Queens Division championship, becoming eligible to play in the city championships at the Garden. The team got to the semifinals, with Cousy leading the scoring, but there it was beaten.

Cousy was named co-captain of the team with Frank Higgins—his old rival—at the start of the 1945-46 season. The team started fast and by midseason was a surefire winner of its second consecutive Queens title. At Jackson there was only one question: Would Cousy win the city scoring title?

All season long, Cousy and Vic Hanson of Long Island City shared the scoring leadership. On the final day of the season, he and Hanson were exactly even in points scored. That afternoon, Hanson scored 21 points. That night, walking out onto the floor to play Far Rockaway, Cousy knew he had to score 22 to win.

He had been averaging only 17 a game; it wasn't too often that he got 20 or more . Since the game meant nothing—Jackson had already won the Queens title—the Jackson players agreed to feed Cousy after they had built up a lead.

The Jackson cheer leaders ripped out one yell after another: "Score, Cousy, Score." As he moved across the floor, Cousy could see the big number 22 in front of him. The ball felt funny in his fingers, and his arms were tight with tension. He took his first shot, missed, and then missed again.

Jackson was building up a safe lead and now the fellows were feeding Cousy. But he kept on missing; as his shots hit the hoop and bounced away, the crowd let out disappointed *ohhhhhhs*. Cousy grimaced, his arms as tight as boards.

At the half he had only 8 points. In the dressing room he took a deep breath, gulping down his disappointment. He had lost his chance to beat Hanson; that was certain. Well, he would have to accept it. Now he would go out there for the second half relaxed and enjoy this game—his last regular-season game for Jackson.

His first shot of the second half went in. He scored again on a drive, the arms feeling loose, the ball spinning cleanly off his fingers. The Jackson players were feeding Cousy on every play now, shouting at him with clenched fists when he scored.

Nobody was keeping track of the teams' scores—Jackson was a runaway winner—but up in the stands they were shouting out Cousy's totals: *Sixteen! Eighteen! Nineteen! Twenty-one!*

Cousy had the ball. He cut, stopped, let go a quick shot. The ball swished through the basket.

The crowd roared and Bob Cousy didn't have to be told that he had just become the New York City scoring champion.

A few weeks later, the New York *Journal-American* picked its All-PSAL team, and Cousy's name led all the rest. The skinny kid with the flowing black hair, who had picked up his first basketball only five years earlier, had been named the best all-around player in the city.

All-City basketball star Cousy sat back, eagerly awaiting the throngs of college coaches who would come pounding at his door, pleading with him to come to their schools.

There were no throngs. For long weeks after the end of the season, not one college coach called Cousy.

CHAPTER 6

A Man Called Doggie

THE phone rang in the Cousy home. Bob answered it. On the other end was Al McClellan, the coach of the Boston College basketball team. He was coming down to New York; he wanted to talk to Bob.

"I'd like to have you and Frank Higgins come back to Boston with me and look over the college," McClellan told Cousy when they met. "I think you'll like it."

Frank Higgins. The boy who had been the best in the schoolyard. Cousy's boyhood idol. They had played together at Jackson, and there were some who thought that Higgins was still a better player than Cousy.

Higgins was still a challenge to Bob, just as Vic Hanson had been a challenge, just as stars like Slater Martin and Oscar Robertson would be challenges later on. As always, Cousy met the challenge. Later he told me how:

"We went up to Boston to try out. Frank was chosen. Although the college also offered to take me, I decided to accept a scholarship from Holy Cross. During the next four years, I played against Frank four times. He developed into a fine ballplayer, but never once did he and Boston College beat Holy Cross."

Higgins became a Boston College all-time great, but Cousy had climbed past his boyhood idol to become an All-American. Cousy thought there was a lesson in his experience for kids.

"Today," he told me, "when I see youngsters idolizing Mickey Mantle—or, I guess, Bob Cousy—I sometimes wonder whether it wouldn't be better if they idolized people they know. Mickey Mantle may be one of the best in baseball, but most youngsters are not likely ever to talk to him, and so he can't be of much help. Instead I would prefer to see my two children model themselves after boys or girls they know, those who are tops in schoolwork or in sports. And then go out and top them."

The call from the Boston College coach had delighted Cousy. It was the first and only call he received from a college coach. The trouble had been his size. At six feet he wasn't big enough for coaches suddenly gone wild over goons. He was a small man in a big man's game.

Boston College, though, was willing to take him. But his visit to the BC campus had disappointed Cousy. The school had no dorms; he would live in a roominghouse near the campus. A roominghouse was not what Cousy had imagined campus life would be like. College, to Cousy, was 1) a place to play basketball; 2) a place to have a gay social life; and 3) a place for learning. And if you had asked him, he would have placed the three in that order.

Shortly after the call from Boston College's McClellan, Cousy heard from Ken Haggerty, a former Andrew Jackson player who was now at Holy Cross, a Catholic college at Worcester, Mass. Haggerty told Cousy about life at Holy Cross—the dorms (Cousy's ears perked), the social life, and an up-and-coming basketball team led by a brilliant coach, Alvin "Doggie" Julian. Haggerty invited Bob to meet Julian when the Holy Cross team came to New York to play Kings Point.

At the game, Cousy was brought to the Holy Cross bench, from where he watched the game. Later he was introduced to Julian.

"I've heard a lot of nice things about you," said Julian.

"Thanks," said Cousy, his face flushing.

So this relationship began on a fine note, a relationship that would later be ruined by foolish mistakes on the part of both Cousy and Julian.

Julian told Cousy that he had been impressed by Bob's good grades. "I don't think you'd have any trouble getting in," said the coach, and Cousy could think gratefully of that forced layoff from basketball in his junior year when he had cracked the books and picked up his marks.

"Are you considering any other college?" asked Julian.

"Well, I'm thinking about Boston College. They've offered me a scholarship."

"What kind?"

"Board, room, tuition and books."

"I think we might do the same for you."

Cousy didn't make any pledges then, but he was Holy Cross's property from that moment on. In talking to his parents later about which school he should pick, Cousy stressed that both schools were equal academically, both were staffed by Jesuits, and that both were Catholic schools (the last two points were especially important to his mother). What he didn't add was how important to him were the dorms and campus life.

Early in September, 1946, Bob Cousy toted heavy suitcases out of his parents' home in St. Albans and took the subway to New York's Grand Central Station, where he would catch another train to Worcester and the hilltop campus of Holy Cross. As Bob rode northward to Worcester, swaying in the seat of a day coach, he thought about what he was leaving behind him—his parents and Joan Kilduff—and he felt the first pangs of homesickness. But then he thought about Bob Cousy coming to Holy Cross and suddenly there were dreams of glory.

Holy Cross had long been one of the weak sisters of college basketball. From 1939 through 1944, for example, the team had managed to win only 22 games. In 1945, Doggie Julian came to Worcester and right away the Cross's basketball fans brightened. Julian brought with him a flock of New York City kids with their brand of give-and-go basketball. There was Joe and Dave Mullaney, George Kaftan, Dermie O'Connell, Ken Haggerty, Charlie Bollinger.

The hustle and spirit of these boys, most of them freshmen in the 1945-46 season, had fired the imaginations of New Englanders, previously as cold as a Maine winter toward this "game for goons." Up to 1945, no college game in Boston had drawn more than 1,500 people. In the winter of 1945-46, Julian's kids from Holy Cross had twice filled the Boston Garden to capacity.

Now, riding on the train toward Worcester, Cousy thought about how he would fit into this young team, seemingly on the edge of greatness. He knew that Julian liked to play with a first and second team, using the second unit to give the regulars a breather. He knew that the first unit in 1945-46 had been O'Connell, Mullaney, Haggerty, Kaftan and Bob Curran.

Five names. Which one would be replaced by Bob Cousy? There was no doubt in Cousy's mind that he would be on that first unit. After all, hadn't he been picked for the New York City All-High School team?

Cousy had—and still has—a thing called confidence. It is an important thing. Warren Spahn has it; you'd see it in the chesty, almost swaggering way he walked out to a mound, as though he were saying: *Nobody's going to beat me today.*

Johnny Unitas has it, too. Once a bunch of the

Colts were sitting around after a practice session before the pro-football season had started. The talk drifted to the rookies who were trying to make the club, and someone wondered which veterans would lose their jobs.

"I'll tell you one thing," said Unitas, speaking in that soft but firm voice, "Otto Graham could be at his best and making a comeback and he wouldn't take *my* job."

Great athletes must have this confidence. Let a pitcher doubt his skills and the fast ball loses its hop, the plate shrinks, the curve ball won't break. Let a quarterback begin to question his accuracy and the ball is as hard to throw as a beachball. Let a basketball player doubt that he will sink a shot and the hoop is no wider than a dime.

You can mistake this confidence for cockiness or conceit or arrogance. Cousy, for instance, was never one to grab your lapels and tell you what a great basketball player he was, but if you asked him, he'd let you know *exactly* how good he was. Once he and some of the other Holy Cross players were watching two pro teams play. One of the pros, Kenny Sailors, threw in a fantastic hook shot.

"Terrific!" yelled Cousy.

Joe Mullaney turned around in his seat, a grin on his face, and asked: "You mean *you* can't make them?"

Cousy smiled softly and said: "Terrific for them, easy for me."

Cousy brought this great faith in himself to the first

Holy Cross practice session. The team worked out in a long narrow barn on the campus; there was barely enough room for ten players to play at one time.

Julian gathered the squad around him for the coach's traditional opening-of-the-season speech. He said he thought the team would have a great year, that he thought the players had learned from last year's youthful mistakes. He went on to say that he figured on using the same system he had used the previous season. There would be two units. The first five would be the regulars from last year's team. The second five would be picked among Andy Laska, Frank Oftring, Charlie Bollinger, Cousy and several other boys.

Cousy's face flushed with anger. Julian hadn't given him a chance to make the team. Now—to make things even worse—he was being told that to make even the second team, he would have to show the goods.

Show the goods! This is Bob Cousy, the best player in New York City, the top scorer in the PSAL. He could have gone to Boston College and played first-string right away. Julian was giving him a raw deal.

Cousy began to sulk at practice sessions. Julian saw that he was sulking, sensed the reason, but said nothing—and even worse, did nothing to explain the situation to Cousy. *A fresh kid, just out of high school, and now he wants to be a regular.*

When the 1946-47 season began, the Holy Cross Crusaders took off like champions. As thousands of shrieking fans jammed Boston Garden, the Cross won its first 10 straight, then 15 straight, then 20 straight—and suddenly they had New Englanders forgetting about clam chowder, Cape Cod, and maybe even Ted Williams.

Cousy was playing with the second unit, usually getting in for a quarter and sometimes even a half. But he burned inside; Julian, he felt, had some personal reason for keeping him off the first unit.

Cousy, of course, was being foolish. He was only a freshman, allowed to play because of wartime rules. He was gaining experience, working well with the second unit, especially with Andy Laska, a slick ball handler. And he finished the season with 227 points, only 10 less than the team's big star—George Kaftan—had scored as a freshman the year before.

But no one explained this to Cousy. And as the season rolled on, he became angrier and angrier. The team won 23 straight, then lost a few, but ended up with a 27-3 record and an invitation to play in the NCAA tournament that would crown the national champion.

Sportswriters called Holy Cross the Cinderella team, for it came out of nowhere—sparked by a great scoring splurge by Kaftan—to topple favorites like Oklahoma and CCNY and win the NCAA title.

Cousy did not feel like a champion. He had played little in the tournament—Julian had to go with his best—and as the team came back to Worcester to be greeted by cheering crowds, Cousy could not feel that the cheers were meant for him.

In the fall of 1947, he came back to school still seething at Julian. But the coach put Bob on the first team, and right away Cousy and Kaftan were the stars of another exciting Crusader team. Cousy began to think he had been wrong about Julian.

And then erupted the explosion.

In midwinter, Loyola of Chicago came to Boston to play Holy Cross. Both teams were rated among the best in the nation. With the game scheduled for Tuesday evening at the Boston Garden, Julian ordered an extra-practice session on the Sunday afternoon before the game.

That Saturday night, Cousy and some friends drove to a dance at a girls' school about a two-hour drive from Worcester. After the dance, they stayed overnight at a hotel, rather than drive back when they were sleepy. On Sunday morning, Cousy got up early, went to Mass, then hopped into the car that would get him back to the campus well before one o'clock, the time practice was to start.

They had been driving for nearly an hour. Suddenly, as the car rounded a curve in the road, it skidded on ice, spun into the other lane, and crashed into an oncoming car.

Steel ground against steel, tires screeched, glass shattered. Shaken, Cousy and his friends climbed out of the car. Surprisingly, nobody had been hurt in either automobile. But Cousy's car had been damaged badly. A long hour went by as he and his friends exchanged names and addresses with the driver of the other car and argued about who would pay for damages. Hasty repairs were made on the car; then they started out again. But they had to move slowly, fearful that the crippled car might conk out. It began to snow, and now the car was barely creeping toward Worcester.

His face flushing with anxiety, Cousy kept looking at his watch. Twelve o'clock, twelve-thirty, one, two, three o'clock. It was past four when the car finally huffed through the gates of the campus. His heart thumping, Cousy leaped out of the car and raced toward the barn. He ran through the door and collided with Father John Devlin, one of the Holy Cross faculty.

"Hello, Bob," said Father Devlin. "We missed you at practice."

Bob tried to twist by him, anxious to get to Julian to explain. "I know, Father," he said.

"What happened?"

Cousy explained hastily. "Gee, Father," he said, "I'm really upset. Is Doggie around?"

"He left some time ago. There's nobody around now."

Bob's knees went weak. "Well, what can I do?"

"I don't think you can do anything. Go up to your room and forget about it and tomorrow you can explain what happened."

But Bob could not forget about it. He slept fitfully that night. The next day he met the team's manager, who asked: "What happened to you?"

Bob told him.

"Have you told Doggie?"

"I haven't seen him. I got back too late yesterday."

"He's wild—mad as hell. He thinks you played in an outside game yesterday."

After classes Cousy searched the campus for Doggie. But by Monday evening, when he reported for practice, the two hadn't met.

Julian ignored Cousy. He ordered two units to scrimmage, but when he called out the lineups, he did not include Cousy. Bob sat on the bench, panic and frustration raging like lions in his chest. Suppose Julian didn't let him play in the game tomorrow night? His whole career ruined—all because of a coach who didn't understand!

Cousy attempted to speak to Julian after practice, but the coach wouldn't listen to him. The next evening —Tuesday—the players piled into the bus that would take them on the two-hour trip to Boston. Cousy tried to sit near Julian, so he could explain, but Doggie surrounded himself with the other players.

Cousy stared moodily out the window as the bus roared down the road toward Boston. He couldn't believe that Julian would keep him out of the lineup. He was the co-star of this team, and this was one of the big games of the season. He'd play a good game tonight and then everything would be OK.

The Boston Garden shook with the roaring of Holy Cross fans. In a bare room underneath the arena, the Holy Cross players put on their uniforms quickly, wisecracking, trying to relax tense nerves. Julian came into the room. He read the starting lineup. Cousy's stomach melted; he wasn't playing.

Cousy watched from the bench, his face pale and taut, as the two teams pounded up and down the court. Here he was, so close to this exciting action and yet not a part of it. Now his temper was beginning to rise, and the more he watched, the angrier he got.

It was a close game, first Holy Cross in the lead, then Loyola. On the bench, the seething Cousy was like a man tied to a tree on a beach, forced to watch his best friend drowning.

Julian had put in other players, but he was humiliating Cousy by making him sit there on the bench, enduring a public punishment for a sin he had not committed. Cousy turned to stare at his tormentor. "The heck with him," he muttered, "I wouldn't go in now if he asked me."

Now there was only a minute left in the half. Julian jumped off the bench. "Cousy!" he yelled.

Cousy stared angrily at Julian. He did not move.

CHAPTER 7

Good-bye to Girls and Holy Cross

IN THE dressing room, Cousy sat alone, near tears. Julian, tight-lipped, would not even look at him.

Cousy knew he had been wrong in refusing to go into the game. Julian was his coach, the boss. He could have fired Bob from the squad right there in Boston Garden.

Cousy cursed himself for his stubbornness. He should have obeyed the order. Now, as the second half was about to begin, he knew that he wasn't likely to get into this game—or maybe any other Holy Cross game.

At the start of the second half, Loyola forged ahead. Up in the stands the crowd was yelling, "Go, Cross, Go," but the Crusaders were running figure-8 patterns without precision, taking shots they shouldn't take, missing easy ones.

With only five minutes left in the game, Loyola had

a 7-point lead. Someone at one end of the arena yelled, "We want Cousy!" and suddenly the chant spread, rocking the Garden: "We want Cousy! We want Cousy!"

Cousy! Cousy! At first it was a plea and then—you could sense the change—it was an angry, insistent demand.

Out on the court, the Holy Cross players looked up, the roar engulfing them. Someone called time out. On the bench, Julian suddenly spun and jerked a finger at Cousy.

Cousy wasn't disobeying this time. He shot to the scorer's table like a man propelled from a gun, the skinny body trembling with energy.

Moments after he got into the game, Cousy shot. He scored. He was a whirling fury, racing up and down the court, grabbing for the ball, shooting and scoring. He drove for a lay-up. He scored. He got the ball again, faked, shot. Two points.

All told he took seven shots in those last few minutes. He sank six for 12 points, enough for a Holy Cross victory.

At the final buzzer, the crowd swept onto the court. Spectators and players pounded Cousy on the back, but he turned and bolted off the court, fleeing wildly toward the dressing room. There he collapsed on a bench, sobbing hysterically, the long thin fingers hiding his face.

Somebody tried to calm him down, but he couldn't stop sobbing, the nervous energy flowing out of him. He ripped off his uniform and staggered into the showers, and there he stayed for a long time, by himself.

He dressed quietly and walked to the bus. He took a seat by himself, staring out the window, speaking to no one, trying to bring his emotions down from that high peak.

He did not speak to Julian that night, nor did he for the rest of the season, except when it was necessary during a game. But Julian kept him on the first unit, and with Cousy going on to score 486 points, then a school record, Holy Cross swept into the NCAA tournament for the second straight year.

This time, though, a fairy godmother did not touch the Cross with her magic wand. In the second game against Kentucky, Cousy missed thirteen out of fourteen shots, and Kentucky ran away with the game. "It took me years," wrote Cousy in his autobiography, "to live down that game."

A few weeks after the game, Cousy was working out in the gym when Julian came by. He called to Cousy, who walked over to where his coach stood.

"Cooz," said Julian, "I've just accepted an offer to coach the Boston Celtics next year."

Cousy looked at him, surprise in his eyes.

Julian hesitated a moment. "I want you to know," he said, "that I'm sorry for anything that might have prevented us from getting along better. It's too bad that there seems to have been a personality clash between us, but now I'd like to shake hands and part friends.

"That's fine with me, Doggie," said Bob, shaking

hands. "I knew there was never anything personal involved, and I guess I did plenty of things I shouldn't have done. I'm sorry about those. But it's all over now."

There was a long silence between these two men, antagonists so long, and then Cousy turned to go back to the court. "Good luck with the Celtics, Doggie," he said.

"Thanks," said Julian, and he walked out of the Holy Cross gym and Cousy's life.

But years later, in 1956, some of Cousy's friends held a banquet for him in Worcester. Julian, then the coach at Dartmouth, was invited, but he couldn't attend. Instead he sent a telegram. It read:

A STREP INFECTION PREVENTS MY JOINING YOU IN LAUDING BOB COUSY, BASKETBALL'S GREATEST. HIS CONTRIBUTION TO BASKETBALL IS NOT ONLY SUPERB PLAY BUT INSPIRATION TO YOUNGSTERS EVERYWHERE WHO ASPIRE TO HIS HEIGHTS. HIS BASKETBALL SUCCESS BELONGS TO BOB HIMSELF, HIS DEVELOPMENT INTO A FINE MAN TO HOLY CROSS COLLEGE. BEST WISHES TO ALL.

"That wire," wrote Cousy in *Basketball Is My Life*, "is one of my proudest possessions."

Growing up in St. Albans, Bob Cousy had a good eye on the basketball court for the basket and a good eye off it for a pretty girl. During his high school days, he dated a girl who kept telling him that someday he would become a great basketball player. Her name was Joan Kilduff, and when all her predictions came true and Bob got the scholarship to Holy Cross, she was delighted.

But during his senior year at Andrew Jackson High School, Cousy's great peripheral vision caught sight of pert and winsome Marie Ritterbusch, a girl everybody called Missie. Bob had played basketball with Missie's brother Ed, but Marie had gone around with an older group than Cousy's friends, and she went to a different school, Bishop McDonnell in Brooklyn. So Cousy didn't see much of her, an omission that he found himself regretting more and more.

In the summer of 1946, before going off to Holy Cross for his freshman year, Cousy learned that a good friend of his, Mike Schmidt, was dating Missie. As smooth in romance as he is in basketball, Bob suggested to Mike that he and Missie double-date with Joan and himself. Mike agreed.

The four double-dated several times that summer, but when Bob went back to Holy Cross, he continued writing letters to Joan. By Christmas, though, when Bob came home for vacation, it was clear to both Bob and Joan that their romance had been only a crush. Joan was interested in somebody else, and so was Bob.

One day he met Missie and they talked for a little while. Then Bob said: "Look, why don't you go out with me some night?"

Missie gave him her pert look. "Because you haven't asked me," she said.

"Well, I'm asking you now."

Bob and Missie dated during the next three years. She came up to Worcester for proms, even for some of the Holy Cross basketball games. During Bob's junior year, they began talking about marriage.

"How about the night of the Junior Prom?" said Bob.

Missie suggested that they wait until Bob had graduated. Reluctantly, Bob agreed.

Then came Bob's senior year—and some Cousy misgivings about marriage. He was now the famous Bob Cousy, the star of the great Holy Cross team. His closest friend at school was another Crusader basketball star, Frank Oftring, and the two soon found that girls all over New England were eager to date them. As far as it was humanly possible, Oftring and Cousy obliged. And the more Cousy dated, pursued by dozens of beautiful girls, the less his thoughts turned to Missie.

One night in the spring of 1950, Bob and Missie began talking about their wedding, which had been set for June, only a few months away. Cousy mentioned how he and Oftring were planning to open a gas station near Worcester in the fall, after they had graduated. He and Oftring had other grandiose plans which they confidently expected would make them millionaires in a few months. Bob talked about these plans with Missie, not mentioning all those adoring females who were pursuing him; then he suggested that with so many important matters on his mind, maybe it would be a good idea to postpone their marriage until the fall.

Missie looked at him, a quizzical look on her face. Then she said: "I was just going to ask you to do that."

Bob's jaw fell. The great Cousy was being spurned. And he didn't like it. "Well," he said, "maybe we ought to get married in June at that."

"Maybe we ought not," said Missie, an edge to her voice. "I don't want to rush into anything."

Now Cousy was angry. He said something, she said something, and in a moment they were shouting at each other, and then Bob walked out of the room, banging the door behind him. The marriage was off, and he didn't care if he ever saw Missie again.

He didn't see her for the rest of the spring. He invited another girl to the Senior Prom. That summer, after graduating, he and Oftring rented a cabin near Worcester, and there were no gayer blades in New England—for a few weeks. And then Cousy began to tire of dating different girls. Bob wasn't hollering it to the skies, but you could tell that he had Missie on his mind. To make things worse, he learned that she was dating another fellow back in St. Albans.

Inside he burned at himself: He could have married Missie in June, and now he'd be the happiest guy on earth. He was a guy aching for his girl to come back, something you could read between the lines of a letter he finally wrote to Missie one day in July.

For 10 long days, there was no answer as Bob waited impatiently, running each morning to the letter box. Finally, early in August, just before his birthday, he got a birthday card from her. On the back of the card was a short note, saying she had taken a job at Winchendon, Mass., about an hour's drive from Worcester.

Cousy made it to Winchendon in thirty minutes. "I was a dope," he said to a somewhat startled Missie. "Please, honey, one more chance."

"One more chance," said Missie.

Three weeks later they were engaged. And in December, 1950, they were married.

When the 1947-48 basketball season ended with the disastrous game against Kentucky, Cousy suddenly found himself studying hard. During his first two years at Holy Cross, Bob had been only a fair student. But now he was becoming aware that he was in college for other things besides basketball.

In his junior and senior years, Bob's average soared into the 90's, even though he was taking tough courses in sociology as well as in his major, business administration. For his senior thesis, he recalled the anti-Semitism that was so rampant in the Yorkville of his childhood and wrote a perceptive paper, "The Persecution of Minority Groups."

With the better grades came more self-assurance off the court. In speeches at pep rallies, he had talked in a stumbling, uncertain manner, nervous about the way he made *r*'s come out as *l*'s. But by the time he was a junior, he could rise at sports banquets and deliver lively speeches with warmth and wit.

In talking to people, he lost what was left of his small-boy shyness, and you didn't feel that half the time Bob Cousy was walking in a world of his own. He was coming out of himself with people, talking to them in a way that made them feel that Bob Cousy would rather be talking to them at this moment than anyone else in the world.

At the start of the 1948-49 season Buster Sheary, who had been Doggie Julian's assistant, became coach of the team. Cousy, Kaftan and the rest of the team were delighted. Everyone liked Sheary, a big, burly, bluff-mannered man who could deliver fire-eating speeches at half time, banging his fists against a wall until they bled. Once he told the players: "Always remember, if you don't want a thing to hurt you, it won't. And if nothing can hurt you, how can anything beat you?"

Under Sheary, the team had a 19-8 record as Cousy, a unanimous All-American, scored 480 points. In the game against Loyola, Cousy had pulled his behind-the-back dribble to win the game in the last few seconds, and now this little team—its biggest man was 6-foot-4—became known around the country as a razzle-dazzle outfit with a touch of magic.

Mostly they ran a figure-8 weave that Doggie Julian had taught them, the ball always in motion and the players seeming to pop out of nowhere, until the defense made a mistake and then it was feed the loose man for a basket.

To the figure-8, a deliberate way of scoring, Holy Cross added the fast break, a bang-bang way of scoring. The fast break had been made popular by West

Coast clubs, but Cousy—first at Holy Cross and later with the Celtics—polished it to perfection.

To start the fast break, an opponent's missed shot is swept off the backboards and passed immediately—with the so-called "outlet" pass—to a guard who has already started to move upcourt. At Holy Cross the guard was Cousy. As he grabbed the outlet pass, Cousy took one quick look, "photographing" in his mind the position of every player behind him. Then with three or four long strides he was past midcourt. Usually it would be a three-on-two fast break, with Cousy and two teammates driving in on two defenders who had managed to get back in time. Sometimes it would be a two-on-one break, with Cousy and a teammate converging on one opponent.

As Cousy drove toward the foul line, his astonishing wide-angle vision would allow him to see Oftring and Kaftan on either side of him. If an opponent moved toward Cousy, *zip* went a pass to whoever was free, and *justlikethat* Holy Cross had scored again.

This was the standard fast break; to it, Cousy added refinements of his own. Sometimes Cousy would drive toward the basket, then flip a pass over his shoulder to a teammate trailing behind him. How did he know the teammate was behind him? Simple. He had taken that mental photograph before the play started. Knowing the speed and habits of his teammates, his brain was able to compute that the player would be in that particular position behind him at that particular time.

Other times Cousy would soar high toward the

basket, and suddenly swing the ball behind his back. *A behind-the-back pass!* thinks his opponent, moving to block the pass.

The pass would never come. Cousy would complete the transfer of the ball behind his back, moving it from his right hand to his left, and then—now all alone—he'd sink an easy lay-up. But other times, just to keep the defense honest, Cousy would sling a behind-the-back pass to Kaftan or Oftring.

His passing became trickier and trickier: bounce passes slapped toward a free man even as Cousy was dribbling; long full-court passes thrown with a windmill motion; short darting passes that sometimes bounced off the skull of the intended receiver, who hadn't been expecting it.

Cousy's magic with a basketball made him and Holy Cross the greatest drawing card in college basketball. When the Crusaders came to play in Boston Garden, capacity crowds filled the huge arena to see this fascinating, heart-stopping team. They'd roar as the poker-faced Cousy would come dribbling downcourt on knotted, muscled legs. He had now reached full size, 6-foot-1, with big hands, wide, sloping shoulders, and long arms.

He could do so many things with a basketball because of his peculiar build, Cousy explained to other players who asked him for his secrets. "If you are physically able to dribble behind your back," he told young players, "it will come to you very easily, just as it came to me that night against Loyola. I didn't have to think about it. I had no other way open, so I had to do it. But it was easy for me because of my long arms. Anyone can do it if you're built like an ape."

More and more coaches were talking about the "ape." "I've seen all of the college stars of this game," said Trinity coach Ray Oesting after Cousy had thrown in 20 points in 20 minutes against his team, "but Cousy is far ahead of anyone."

"I see it," said another coach. "But I don't believe it."

But Cousy had more than a marvelous physique and a repertoire of tricky moves. He brought to basketball a raging spirit to win. In the Sugar Bowl tournament in the 1948-49 season, Holy Cross finished fourth by losing in the semifinals and again in the consolation game. But Cousy had been the outstanding player of the tournament. He came out to center court to receive a silver mug, and when he did, the huge crowd rose and applauded.

He stood there, the sweat running down the skinny body. And suddenly he was sobbing, the body heaving, and the cheering grew louder.

"Look at him," said somebody on the sideline. "Those cheers—they made the kid bawl, he's so grateful."

"Grateful, nothing," said a Boston sportswriter. "He's crying because he's mad we lost."

Cousy had less reason to cry in his senior year, the season of 1949-50. The team, a seasoned bunch led by Cousy and Oftring, got off to a whirlwind start, winning its first 10, then 15, and now it was 20 in a row and on the Holy Cross campus all you heard was talk about Cousy and "the team."

George Kaftan had graduated a year earlier. The two had not been the closest of friends, different in temperament and perhaps more than a little jealous of the other's publicity. Kaftan graduated at midterm in the 1948-49 season. His last game was against Springfield. Near the end of the game, with the Cross way ahead, Cousy drove for a basket with Kaftan behind him. Without thinking to pass to Kaftan so that he could finish his career with a basket, Cousy shot and scored.

Kaftan looked at Bob, his face angry. "For the love of Mike," he said to the greatest passer of all time, "don't you ever pass?"

And so a great partnership ended.

The team rolled on without Kaftan. The biggest man was still only 6-foot-4, but the Crusaders knocked off giant after giant, rolling up 26 straight victories, until along came little Columbia.

Playing Holy Cross on the Columbia court, the Lions pulled off the biggest upset of the year, beating the Crusaders and ending the streak. Holy Cross finished the season at 27-2, but the edge had come off the team. In the opening round of the NCAA tournament, North Carolina State ended Cousy's career at Holy Cross with a defeat.

Cousy and the team went back home to Worcester with hangdog looks. They were met by cheering mobs of students, who applauded this team that had kept the school—and the country—transfixed through a 26-

game winning streak. And school officials announced that Cousy's number 17 would be retired, the first time Holy Cross had ever retired a basketball player's number.

Happy, Cousy went back to his books and preparation for final exams—but he had one eye on a man named Walter Brown.

CHAPTER 8

"Cousy's a Bum"

WHEN he was studying at Holy Cross one day during the spring of 1950, Cousy got a phone call from a Boston newspaperman.

"What's your reaction to the news, Bob?" asked the writer.

"What news?"

"Haven't you heard? The Celtics didn't take you."

"Who did?"

"Tri-Cities."

"Who?"

The reporter was talking about the National Basketball Association draft meeting, held earlier that day. Once a year, the NBA owners meet to select the best of the college basketball players. Cousy had hoped that Walter Brown, the co-owner of the Boston Celtics, would pick him, since Bob and Missie had decided they would like to live in Worcester, which is only two hours from Boston. Cousy had formed many friendships in Worcester while at Holy Cross. Moreover, Bob had made his reputation in New England; he figured there would be many more business opportunities for him if he kept on playing basketball there.

After the reporter hung up, Cousy did some inquiring. He found that Tri-Cities was an NBA team representing Moline and Rock Island in Illinois, and Davenport, Iowa. Illinois and Iowa! They were a long way from Worcester.

The next day the Boston newspapermen, to whom Cousy was next to divine, swarmed angrily into the Celtics' offices to interview Brown and his new coach, Arnold "Red" Auerbach (who had succeeded Doggie Julian). Brown explained that the Celtics needed a big man; thus they had drafted 6-foot-11 Charlie Share of Bowling Green. "I wish we could have gotten both Cousy and Share," Brown told the reporters. "But it wasn't possible. Tri-Cities picked Bob before we could get him in the second round."

The reporters weren't mollified. They turned angrily to Auerbach, and asked: "Why didn't you make Cousy your first draft choice?"

Auerbach turned to Brown. "Am I supposed to win," he snapped, "or worry about playing the local yokels?"

And Brown, looking at his shoes, said: "Just win."

Cousy signed with Tri-Cities before the start of the 1950-51 season, but never even practiced with the team, which traded him to the Chicago Stags. *That* team folded just before the season began. The Chicago players were parceled around the league, but three remained to be divided among Boston, New York and Philadelphia. The three players were sharpshooting Max Zaslofsky, playmaker Andy Phillip, and Cousy.

All three ciubs wanted Zaslofsky. The second choice was Phillip. Nobody wanted Cousy.

The three club owners met in New York to decide who would get Max. The president of the NBA, Maurice Podoloff, sat down in a hotel room with Boston's Walter Brown, New York's Ned Irish, and Philadelphia's Eddie Gottlieb. For hours they argued in the hotel room. It was near midnight when Podoloff suddenly threw up his hands.

"I've had enough of this," he said. "I'm going to put the three names in a hat. Each of you draw. The player you pick, that's the one you get."

He wrote the three names on three slips of paper and dropped them into a hat. Walter Brown said, "I'll pick first." He stuck his hand into the hat.

Cousy was at his mother's home in St. Albans when the telephone rang. It was a little after midnight. Sleepily, Bob picked up the phone.

"Bob?"

Cousy recognized the voice; it was Walter Brown's.

"Yeah," said Cousy, his heart beginning to race.

"Walter Brown. Get in your car and drive back to Boston. You're with us."

Cousy let out a loud whoop. He didn't know how it had all happened; no one had told him he had been traded by Tri-Cities. He had been expecting a call from the owner of the Tri-Cities team, ordering him to fly out to Davenport or Moline or something.

The next afternoon, Bob was back in Boston. There he picked up the afternoon papers and learned that New York had been the lucky team; it had picked Zaslofsky, with Phillip going to the Warriors. And for years, Ned Irish and Eddie Gottlieb would shake their heads thinking how easily they once could have had Bob Cousy.

The Boston newspapers had some other news for Cousy. "Cousy," Red Auerbach was quoted as saying, "is going to have to make this club."

Later that afternoon Bob met Auerbach for the first time. A tough-talking, cigar-chomping man with cold, piercing eyes, Auerbach looks upon the world with suspicion, as though it were populated only by his enemies. He walks with a watchful eye, certain that someone is going to knife him at any moment. He does not make many friends and he prefers it that way. But when he has a friend—as Cousy became after many years—the relationship can be as deep and warm as the love between brothers.

"I hope you can make the team," Auerbach told Bob in a brisk voice. "If you can, I'll be glad to have you. But if you can't, don't blame me. A little guy always had two strikes on him in this business. It's a big man's game."

Actually Boston was hardly the toughest team in the NBA to make. During the previous season, it had finished dead last in the Eastern Division, winning only 22 of its 68 games. But it had tried—and rejected

—some good college ballplayers, including three hot shots from Holy Cross: George Kaftan, Dermie O'Connell, and Joe Mullaney.

And after Bones McKinney, a veteran NBA player, saw Cousy for the first time, he said: "If he keeps on making the mistakes I've seen him pull, the pros will make him just one more All-American bust."

Cousy made many of his mistakes on defense. After one game, Auerbach told a reporter: "He shot all right, but I think he gave away two points on defense for every one he scored."

The Boston reporters didn't like hearing that kind of talk about their idol, but dutifully they printed each Auerbach blast at the Cooz. And the next morning, the Cooz would pick up the paper, read the blast, and mentally poleax Auerbach.

But the next time he played, he'd grit his teeth and concentrate harder on defense.

After one game in which Cousy's defensive work was above reproach, the reporters trooped into the dressing room, big grins on their faces. Well, they said to Auerbach, wasn't Cousy great tonight on defense?

"So-so," said Auerbach. "But those fancy passes he threw away. They came near to losing the game for us."

And again the reporters would print the Auerbach quotes. And again Cousy would read them, the fires rising within him: *I'll show that guy, I'll show him.* . . .

Once, watching Cousy gnash his teeth while reading

an Auerbach blast, a reporter turned to the coach and said: "Why are you keeping Cousy so mad at you?"

Auerbach only grinned.

Cousy's tricky passes sometimes did fool his own teammates. In one memorable game, a behind-the-back pass smacked big Ed Macauley on the back of the head.

After the game Auerbach talked with Cousy. "Bob," he said, "you're losing the ball for us with that fancy stuff."

"That's not my fault, Arnold," said Bob. "There's nothing wrong with most of my passes. It's just that the fellows aren't expecting them. I believe that when your team has the ball, you should know where the ball is at all times. And you should be expecting a pass at all times."

Gradually, Easy Ed and the rest began to expect Cousy's passes. And with Cousy passing and scoring with hook shots from every possible angle, the Celtics suddenly became contenders. By midseason they were battling Philadelphia for first place. On January 14, 1951, the two teams met at the Boston Garden with the top spot on the line.

Cousy was hot. And so was Easy Ed Macauley, throwing in soft hooks from the pivot. Chuck Cooper was driving underneath, pulling off rebounds. But Philadelphia kept pace, with Jumping Joe Fulks—the first of the jump-shot artists—and George Senesky and Paul Arizin pouring in baskets from inside and outside.

With a minute to go, Boston led by four points. The Celtics called time out.

Auerbach gathered the players around him and then he said what he would say so many times over the next 12 years: "Give the ball to Cousy."

Cousy got the ball. He began to dribble. As long as he kept the ball moving, he could not be called for "freezing," which was against NBA rules. The Warriors chased after him, frantically trying to grab that bouncing ball. Philadelphia's Nelson Bobb lunged at the Cooz.

Foul! Cousy calmly went to the foul line and sank the shot.

The Warriors came upcourt, missed the shot, and again here was the Cooz with the ball. *Bam! Bam! Bam!* the dribbling ball smacked against the floor. A player dived at Cousy, the ball went *bambambambam,* and Cousy was loose again.

Again he was fouled. And again he made the shot.

Five times Cousy walked to the line and sank the foul shot. The Warriors were still chasing Cousy when the buzzer sounded with the Celtics ahead, 97-87. Cousy had scored 34 points.

The Warriors filed into their dressing room, heads down, snarling. Plump Eddie Gottlieb pulled the cigar out of his mouth and yelled at reporters: "Sure, Bob Cousy's great. He can freeze the ball. But I question whether it helps the league."

Leo Mogus, a player, put it another way: "Bush league, that's what it was, bush."

Over in the Celtics' dressing room, Cousy sat with

sweat streaming down his dark, pointed face. He laughed when someone told him what Mogus had said. "They get paid for playing their way," he said, "and I do the same here. Auerbach likes me to dribble. When he tells me to stop, then I'll stop."

But the Warriors had been made to look bad. A writer reminded Cousy what Auerbach had said a few days earlier: "If you show up a professional basketball player, look out. The next time he'll put you in the second gallery."

Cousy grinned, thinking of his battle to make this team. "If that's all I had to worry about," he said, "I'd be in good shape."

The next time Philadelphia played Boston, nobody put Bob Cousy in the second balcony. He led the way as the Celtics routed Philadelphia, 98-73.

As the Celtics hung on to first place, it was obvious that Bob Cousy had made the team. By midseason, in fact, it was obvious that he had become an NBA All-Star in this, his rookie year. Paul Birch, the coach of the Fort Wayne team, told reporters how Cousy had broken open a game against his club in one 25-second burst. Cousy had thrown in a 20-foot set shot, dribbled through the entire Fort Wayne team for a score, then grabbed a rebound and threw a court-length pass to a teammate for another two points.

"I've never seen his equal," said Birch. "Cousy scored thirty-two points against us the last time and I thought the man guarding him played a pretty good game."

Even one-time skeptic Bones McKinney was won

over. "Who ever heard of a great scorer being at the same time great at assists? Tremendous!"

What McKinney meant was this: While Cousy was ninth in the league in scoring in only his first year, he was also assisting teammates to score with passes. He finished second in the league in number of assists.

But the Celtics couldn't hold on to first place, finishing second to Philadelphia. The NBA, though, has a strange way of determining its champion. At the end of the regular season, the team that finishes first in the Eastern Division does *not* meet the team that finishes first in the Western Division in a World Series for the championship.

No, that would be too simple. And with such an arrangement, the other NBA teams would not make as much money.

What happens is this: The team that finishes second in its division meets the third-place team in a short series. The winner then plays the first-place team in a longer series. That winner is crowned division champion. It then meets the other division champion in a best-of-seven series for the NBA championship.

Thus, oddly enough, a team can play a full 82-game schedule, finish in first place far ahead of the second-place team, but lose one series and be out of the running for the championship.

In 1950-51, Cousy's rookie year, the second-place Celtics met New York, the third-place team, in the opening series for the Eastern Division title. New York won in two games—and so began for Cousy and the Celtics six long years of frustration.

In 1951-52, the Celtics were second again—this time only a game behind the Syracuse Nationals. But again New York beat Boston in the opening play-off.

In the 1952-53 season, Auerbach obtained backcourt help for Cousy: hard-driving, husky Bill ("Willie") Sharman, who could run with Cousy on the fast break and snare his sudden passes. Just as important, he had a sharpshooter's eye, especially from the foul line.

Enthusiasm blazed high in Boston: this would be the year the Celtics would go all the way.

For the second straight year, Cousy finished third behind the two giants—Minneapolis's 6-foot-9 George Mikan and Philadelphia's 6-foot-8 Neil Johnston—in scoring, averaging 19 points a game. He led the league in assists. The Celtics were third in the Eastern Division. In the opening play-off series, they were matched against the second-place Syracuse Nats.

Boston won the first game of the best-of-three series. The second game was played at the Boston Garden; a full house looked on, hungry to see the Celtics knock their old nemesis, Syracuse, out of the play-offs.

Cousy was playing on a bad leg and you could see that his slowness was a brake on the Celtic attack. With less than a minute to go, the Nats led, 77-76. Cousy came down with the ball, saw a Celtic open under the basket. He threw, but the pass was a wild one. The Nats had the ball and Cousy was wearing goat's horns.

A few moments later, though, the Celtics got the ball back. Cousy was fouled. Calmly, with everything riding on the shot, he went to the foul line. The Garden went quiet. Cousy bounced the ball, took a deep breath, hesitated, then shot. The ball swished through, the score was tied, 77-77, and the game went into overtime. It was Cousy's 25th point of the night.

In the first overtime, Cousy threw in 6 of the 9 Celtic points, including a last-second free throw that tied the score and sent the game into a second five-minute overtime. With seconds remaining of the overtime and Syracuse leading, 90-88, Cousy sank a desperation shot and the game went into the third overtime.

With 18 seconds left, the Celtics were trailing by two points. Cousy was fouled. He walked to the line, weary now, the breath coming hard and dry, the pressure still on him, but in the deathly quiet of the Garden he sank both foul shots to tie the score.

Now Syracuse had the ball. The Nats froze the ball until the last few moments, and with three seconds left, they hit for two points. Cousy grabbed the ball, raced downcourt, and threw in a 25-foot push shot as the buzzer sounded. Again the game was tied.

In the fourth overtime period, Syracuse built up a quick five-point lead, but then Cousy hit for nine of 12 Celtic points and Boston was the winner, 111-105.

The crowd spilled onto the floor, carrying Cousy off, and it wasn't till later that the statisticians figured it all out: Cousy had hit for 25 points in the four overtimes for a total of 50 points, an NBA record at the time. Even more amazing, he had sunk 30 free throws in 32 tries—18 of them in succession during the four pressure-packed overtimes.

In Boston they still call it Cousy's greatest game.

But in Boston a week later, they were calling Cousy and the Celtics other things. After having beaten the Nats, the Celtics met the Knicks for the Eastern Division title. The Knicks swamped the Celtics in four straight games.

The 1953-54 Celtics started out like winners, beating everybody in sight. Then came a slump and in mid-December the Celtics were routed by the Warriors in a game at the Garden. Cousy had been miserable, taking all kinds of shots and coming up with a puny four points.

Cousy drove home to Worcester that night, figuring it had just been one of those days. "You get into a slump," he once said, "and you have to get your confidence back. I get mine back by sinking the easiest lay-ups I can get, driving in as close as I can get to the basket and sinking an easy shot. Then, when you feel you have the touch again, you can start moving back, taking longer shots, and after a while you get the feeling that every little old thing you throw up there will go in—until your next slump. One good thing about basketball slumps, though—they never last more than a game or two."

Walter Brown and Red Auerbach, however, were not so philosophical when they got up to speak the next afternoon at a basketball luncheon in Boston. Memories are short in sports; both had obviously forgotten about the greatness of the Cooz in the Syracuse play-off game less than a year earlier.

Auerbach let go the first blast. "We're playing lousy

ball," he said, "and I know why. Macauley just isn't tough enough underneath. Sharman has got to stop looking for shots all the time. Cousy controls the ball and it's up to him to let the cornermen make the plays, not try to do it all himself."

Then Brown got up to add his piece. He was spending a lot of money on this team, he said, but if he had to spend a lot of money, he would rather spend it on a winner than on a loser. "Some of our stars," said the ruddy-faced Irishman, "are going to be playing for less salary unless we get up where we belong in the standings."

He pounded a fist against the table. "And that doesn't mean just beating out Syracuse for second place in our division."

Later there was other talk: that Cousy might be traded. And at the tables the people said maybe that was a good idea. "Brown's right," said a reporter. "Cousy's a bum." Others nodded, the same ones who had cheered so loudly the previous March when Cousy had single-handedly defeated Syracuse in the four overtimes.

Back in Worcester, Cousy's phone began to ring. Reporters asked for his comment on the blast.

"What blast?" asked Bob.

The reporters told him what had been said at the luncheon. And now the Cousy temper flared.

That night he appeared on a Worcester radio show. "I don't understand this trade talk," he said. "I'm pretty upset about it. I don't understand why those statements about me were made at the luncheon in

Boston today. If the Celtics aren't satisfied with my playing, I want to be traded."

But that night, Cousy tossed restlessly in bed. He wanted to stay with the Celtics. He couldn't play anywhere else except in New England.

Maybe he had said too much. Maybe Brown and Auerbach would let him go. If they did, he'd have to quit this game he loved so much. He'd have to quit.

CHAPTER 9

"A Winner at Last"

THE COOZ slumped on the bed in the Minneapolis hotel room, wondering what he would say when he met Auerbach. Bob had flown alone from Worcester to Minneapolis. The rest of the team, including Auerbach, would be arriving within a few minutes. Cousy had wanted to be alone to unscramble his emotions. But now—as he sat on the bed with his hands clasped—he was still as confused as he had been the night before, when he had tossed in bed, fearful he had said too much.

Back in Boston, Walter Brown was talking to a reporter. "The first thing we've got to do," he said, "is square ourselves with Cousy."

The phone rang at Cousy's elbow. On the other end was Auerbach. He had just arrived with the team and was down in the lobby.

"Can I come up?" said Auerbach. "I want to talk to you."

Of course Auerbach could come up. Bob put down the phone. His stomach began to seesaw.

Auerbach came into the room, his eyes appraising. "Lots of excitement yesterday," he said.

"I'll say."

Auerbach took out a cigar and stared at it. "Look," he said, "nobody wants to trade you. Get that straight."

Cousy nodded. There was relief on his face. They talked for several hours about the team: its strength, its weaknesses, how the club could be improved.

When Auerbach left the room, the air had been cleared between Cousy and the Celtics. Perhaps for the first time, the Celtics realized how important this skinny guy was to the club. And also perhaps for the first time, this skinny guy realized how important the Celtics were to him.

There would be other hot words between Cousy and Auerbach over the years. But they would be the hot words of a family argument, soon forgotten and leaving no wounds. Nobody had said anything official, but it was clear that never again would any Celtic official talk about trading Cousy. He was part of the family now.

Cousy walked through the door marked ATHLETES ENTER HERE. He descended a staircase that spiraled downward into the basement caverns of Madison Square Garden. He walked into a bare, steamy room where nine of the greatest basketball players in the world were sitting.

This was the dressing room of the Eastern All-Stars. A few yards down the dark hallway, inside another room, sat ten other men, the best of the West. In a little while they would meet on brightly lit, yellow-stained boards to play the 1954 NBA All-Star game before more than 16,000 howling New Yorkers.

Cousy wanted to do well. This was Madison Square Garden, where he had played for Andrew Jackson nearly a decade earlier. This was his hometown. "I like to play well in New York," he said later. "They know when you're doing a good job and when you're doing a bad job, and they let you know."

Cousy undressed slowly, the preoccupied look on his face, a glaze coming over his eyes, the rage to win building up inside him. Around him the other players shouted wisecracks at each other: New York's little Dick McGuire, a guard almost as tricky as Cousy; Syracuse's big and powerful Dolph Schayes, who could battle under the boards and shoot long arching set shots from outside; big-jawed Neil Johnston from the Warriors, who wheeled gracefully from the pivot to throw in hook shots with the ease of a man dropping fish down a barrel. There was Easy Ed Macauley and Willie Sharman from the Celtics and the strapping Harry "the Horse" Gallatin of the Knicks.

And in that other room, where the West team was dressing, there were ten men who many thought were the best basketball team ever assembled under one roof: mountainous 6-foot-9 George Mikan, the greatest scorer of his time; his Minneapolis teammate, towering Jim Pollard, who combined with Mikan to give the Lakers domination in scoring and rebounding, a domination that would result in three straight NBA championships. There was Fort Wayne's burly, high-scoring Larry Faust; slick backcourtmen Bobby Wanzer and Bob Davies, both from Rochester; and Minneapolis's 5-foot-10 guard, Slater "Dugie" Martin, famous for his ability to guard the Cooz.

On this night at Madison Square Garden, though, Martin could not hold Cousy as Bob worked backcourt magic with his partner, tricky Dick McGuire. Cousy and McGuire kept feeding the big men, Gallatin and Johnston, then shooting over the defense when it tried to collapse around the pivot men. Big Jim Pollard was scoring for the West, but with less than a minute to go the East led, 82-80.

At the press table, an NBA official began balloting the reporters to pick the Most Valuable Player. The winner was Jim Pollard, who had played such a fine game in a losing cause.

Out on the court, the East had the ball, and Cousy was dribbling at center court, running out the clock. One West player dived at Cousy, but the Cooz slipped away, and then—

Swish! Bob Davies had stolen the ball from Cousy. He raced downcourt, all alone, leaped and scored. The West had tied the score. As writer Steve Gelman put it later in his book, *Bob Cousy, Magician of Pro Basketball*: "Bob Davies . . . had upstaged the Cooz."

Cousy came upcourt with the ball, his face still impassive. To look at him, you could never have told that he had just been made the goat of the game. Cousy dribbled the ball across midcourt to the top of the circle, then took a quick look at the clock. Ten seconds, eight seconds . . . and suddenly Cousy was driving, leaping high over Martin and unleashing a right-handed hook shot. . . .

High above the Garden in a radio booth, a sports announcer—shouting to make himself heard above the roaring of the crowd—screamed into the microphone, his voice splitting: "It's GOOD!"

The Cooz had come back to put the East ahead, 84-82. But with only three seconds to go, big George Mikan was fouled. He calmly sank both shots and the game went into overtime.

On the first play, Cousy threw in a long set shot. He took a pass from McGuire, feinted, then threw in a one-hander. He sank a foul shot, then passed to Willie Sharman, who scored. He thread-needled a pass into Neil Johnston, who wheeled off the pivot and sank a hook shot. He drove past Martin and scored. He threw in a running one-hander for another two points.

The East was home free, winning 98-93 in the overtime. And at the press table the writers were scratching out the name of Jim Pollard on their ballots. The new winner of the MVP trophy was Bob Cousy.

Years later he told me: "As far as personal achievement is concerned, I think I got my biggest thrill at the 1954 All-Star game. It was played at Madison Square Garden, and I have always liked to do well at the Garden, New York being my hometown. But more than that, the trophy meant a lot to me because they had picked another man, and then we came back to win it. That's the way you like to win."

Somehow, though, the Celtics couldn't win the big play-off games. And in Boston there was grumbling that the Celtics choked up. "They can't win the big ones," said basketball fans as they streamed sadly out of Boston Garden after seeing the Celtics knocked out of another play-off.

In the 1953-54 season, Cousy was second in the league in scoring and tops in assists. But Syracuse swept by them in two games to win the Eastern title. Minneapolis beat the Nats for the NBA championship.

In 1954-55, Cousy was third in the league in scoring and again tops in assists. Boston finished third and beat New York in the opening play-offs. But in the big series for the Eastern title, Syracuse beat the Celtics easily in four straight games (and then went on to defeat Fort Wayne for the championship).

In 1955-56, Cousy was seventh in scoring and again the leader in assists. The Celtics finished second to Philadelphia in the regular season, but in the opening play-off, it was the same old story: Syracuse beat them. Philadelphia went on to win the Eastern title and the championship.

Early in 1956, Red Auerbach told a group of reporters why he thought the Celtics couldn't win the crucial play-off games. He pointed a finger at Easy Ed Macauley, who was taking practice shots out on the court. "He is the gamest, hardest-working guy I know," said Auerbach. "But he's not strong enough to battle under the boards. The poor cuss doesn't weigh 180 pounds."

With Macauley not getting enough rebounds, Cousy wasn't getting the ball often enough to trigger a fast break. And without the ball, you can't score.

In 1956, Brown and Auerbach took a gamble. They traded away Macauley and Cliff Hagan, two proven pros, for a kid who had never played a minute of pro basketball. In fact, the Celtics weren't even sure he wanted to play in the NBA.

The kid's name was Bill Russell, a 6-foot-11 center whose rebounding had made the University of San Francisco the best of the college teams in the 1955-56 season. A unanimous All-American, Russell was picked for the 1956 U. S. Olympic team. As the 1956-57 NBA season began, he was playing for Uncle Sam's basketball team in the Olympics at Melbourne, Australia. In between Olympic games he was mulling over two offers: to make a lot of money cavorting with the Harlem Globetrotters, or to make less money but gain a lot of prestige playing in the NBA with the Celtics.

While Walter Brown wooed the big guy long-distance, the Celtics were starting the season with a zip. Cousy and Willie Sharman were working their usual miracles in the backcourt, and Auerbach had obtained the veteran Andy Phillip to back them up. The centers were two huge men, 6-foot-9 Arnie Risen and 6-foot-7 Jack Nichols.

The forwards were powerful "Jungle Jim" Loscutoff, a 6-foot-5 heavyweight who knew how to throw his weight around when the other team got too rough. The Celtics called him their "policeman." The other forward was a rookie from Bob's alma mater, Holy Cross, a big grinning kid named Tommy Heinsohn. Later the Celtics would nickname him "The Gunner," because when Heinsohn got a hand on the ball, the result was inevitable: a jump shot at the basket. But the Celtics didn't mind because The Gunner was hitting at an astounding percentage for a rookie—40 percent.

The Celtics had another rookie that year, a somber-faced boy with a crew cut and a drawl—Kentucky All-American Frank Ramsey. He didn't get to play too much in 1955-56, but he would go on to become the Celtics' most versatile player. Often in a third or fourth period, Auerbach would put Ramsey into the game, sometimes in the backcourt, sometimes in the corners. But wherever he played, Ramsey had a knack for going on a five-minute scoring splurge, scoring five or six quick baskets that would break a close game wide open.

By December the Celtics were in first place, four games ahead, and then came trouble. Risen broke his arm; the big center would be out for most of the season. Cousy had a pulled leg muscle and was limping. Loscutoff was hurt.

To the rescue came Walter Brown. His long-distance entreaties had paid off: big Bill Russell had signed with the Celtics.

Auerbach was exultant. "This club at full strength," he told a reporter, "is the answer to a coach's dream. We've got the same backcourt strength we've always had with Cousy and Sharman, we're stronger than we've ever been up front, and we've got good depth everywhere. Heinsohn and Loscutoff are powerfully built boys who can get rebounds, and Russell is going to be the best center in the business."

Springing his 6-foot-11 frame off the floor like a missile off a launching pad, Russell would go high above everybody else to snare a rebound. Then, twisting as he came down, he'd sling the ball to Cousy, who'd have the ball before big Bill had hit the ground. And then Cousy was off and running, with Sharman and Heinsohn trailing him, sweeping down on the defense before it could organize, firing a variety of passes that bewildered opponents.

Soon the entire nation was talking about this exciting team. Russell's first game was seen on a national TV network, and few basketball games ever had a more exciting and incredible finish.

With seven seconds to go, Boston trailed St. Louis by three points. The Celtics had the ball out of bounds. The Celtics had a play set up: Cousy was supposed to pass in to Sharman, who would drive and try to be fouled as he shot. If he sank the shot and was fouled, he would score three points and tie the game.

But St. Louis's Easy Ed Macauley, who was guarding Tommy Heinsohn, recognized the play from his old days as a Celtic. He began to move toward Sharman. Seeing Macauley move, Slater Martin—who was guarding Cousy—shouted: "Ed, be careful!"

The shout made Macauley's head turn—for just an instant. And in that instant, Cousy lined the ball to Heinsohn, who dunked an easy shot.

But still the Celtics were behind by one; there were only six seconds left and the Hawks had the ball. But as St. Louis came up with the ball, a pass went astray; the Celtics had it again with three seconds left.

Again the Celtics lined up for an out-of-bounds play. This time Cousy fired the pass to Sharman, who turned and got off a quick one-hander. The ball swished through the nets as the buzzer sounded. The Celtics ran off the court the winners while millions at home shook their heads and said, "Did you *ever* see anything like it?"

The NBA had never seen anything like it, either, as this whirlwind team finished first in the Eastern Division by six games, then knocked off its old nemesis—Syracuse—to become Eastern champions.

Champions of the West were the St. Louis Hawks. The Hawks were built around gangly 6-foot-9 Bob Pettit, a tremendous shooter who could score from outside with long one-handers or tap in rebounds from under the boards. He had finished second in the league in scoring, averaging almost 25 points a game.

At the corners were Easy Ed Macauley and sharp-shooting Jack Coleman. In the backcourt was the old Celtic, Cliff Hagan, who had become one of the league's All-Stars.

The other backcourtman was the ex-Laker, Slater "Dugie" Martin. Years later Cousy would say that nobody could guard him as well for a short time as Syracuse's Larry Costello; but over an entire game, said Bob, no one covered him with the tenacity of Martin. That wasn't too surprising, since Martin was much like Cousy in temperament, with a fierce, hungry desire to win.

The two teams met at Boston Garden for the first game of the best-of-seven series for the NBA championship. Though Cousy and Sharman scored 62 points between them, the Hawks won in two overtimes, 125-123. But the Celtics evened the series by winning the second game, 119-99, with Cousy scoring 22.

The two teams flew to St. Louis for the third and fourth games. With 44 seconds left in the third game, Pettit popped in a long jumper and the Hawks won, 100-98. But again the Celtics evened the series by winning the fourth game, 123-118. In that game, Cousy scored 31. Dugie Martin's total: 15.

The Celtics won the fifth game, 124-109, but the Hawks took the sixth, 96-94 (Hagan tapped in a rebound with seconds remaining). And now the two teams came together at Boston Garden, before a house filled with screaming Boston fans, for the seventh and decisive game.

Before the game, the sportswriters filled their stories with speculation about Cousy and Sharman, who had been off in their shooting during the last two games. Would the two get hot in this final game?

In the opening minutes, the Boston fans shrieked at Cousy to sink one. But the Cooz, his face still that expressionless mask, could not buy a basket. Neither could Sharman.

Heinsohn and Russell were scoring, but at the half the Hawks led by two. In the dressing room, Cousy sat on a bench, holding his head, disgusted with himself. But Auerbach made it clear that he was sticking with Cousy and Sharman. They had brought the team this far, to this point so close to the championship that Boston had dreamed of for so long. Auerbach wasn't going to give up on them now. Class, he told the Celtics, would tell.

In the third period, Heinsohn could hardly miss, and the Celtics went ahead by six. But back came Pettit to tie the score, and then the Hawks forged ahead. Now, with less than a minute to go and a championship at stake, the Hawks were ahead by two.

The Garden was one huge cavern of noise as the Celtics came up with the ball. Ramsey had the ball near the key. He shot. *Good!* And the game went into overtime.

With less than a minute left of the overtime, the Celtics led by one. Cousy was fouled. He went to the line for two shots, and suddenly the Garden went still. He made the first shot; a great burst of sound shattered the Garden.

Now he stood on the line again. If he sank this shot, the Celtics were ahead by three, a decisive margin with so few seconds left. Cousy bounced the ball, once, twice, took a deep breath to relax the muscles, then shot.

The ball hit the front rim, then bounced away. The Hawks grabbed it and stormed downcourt. Someone shot.

Two points! The score was tied. Heinsohn drove and scored with 15 seconds left, and the huge crowd screamed and stomped its feet. The Celtics were ahead.

Back came the Hawks in those last few moments. Coleman shot. *Good!* The score was tied again. Moments later the buzzer cut through the roaring. Second overtime.

Up in the stands hands shook trying to light cigarettes. Hearts pounded, nerves twitched. To come so near to a championship, people were thinking, to come so near and then to lose it. The prospect seemed unendurable. If the Celtics could win, Boston fans would ride home in sunshine; if the Celtics lost, they would go home filled with cold and black despair.

The second five-minute agony began, the players streaming sweat, open mouths sucking for air, the legs aching, muscles sore with fatigue. Heinsohn fouled out. He staggered to the bench, tears running down his face, and buried his head in a towel, near hysteria. He had scored 37 points and the crowd gave him a standing ovation.

With less than a minute to go, the Celtics led by one, 124-123, and they had the ball. Jim Loscutoff drove for a lay-up and was fouled.

The Garden was quiet as Loscutoff stood on the line. He shot. The ball snapped through the cords and that sudden, happy shout of the crowd might have been heard all the way to Cape Cod.

Behind 125-123 with seconds left, the Hawks' playing coach, Alex Hannum, called time out. He gathered his players around him and ordered a special play.

The whistle blew. Play was about to start. Up in the stands, 13,000 Celtic fans leaned forward, breathing hard, wringing scorecards in wet hands.

Now Hannum had the ball. He threw a long pass right at the backboard, just as Pettit—the scoring hero of the play-offs—cut underneath.

The ball smacked into the backboard as Pettit leaped high into the air, his big hands reaching to tap the ricochet into the basket. Below him—mouths wide—the Celtics watched, afraid to foul him and give the Hawks the three-point play that would win the game.

The ball ricocheted off the backboard right into Pettit's flashing fingers. He tapped it back. The ball hit the rim, spun around and out. The buzzer sounded. The Celtics were champions.

Out they came from the stands, yelling and cheering, some of them crying. Heinsohn was lifted up on shoulders, then Auerbach, and then they were yelling for the captain of the team, Cooz. He had hit only two field goals in this game, but he had hit a thousand and more in the long seven years before this championship, and Boston had not forgotten.

Up went Cousy and he was shaking hands, tears in

his eyes. Later, in the dressing room, he would hug Auerbach, who had built this team, and Walter Brown, who had risked so much money on it. And later still he would sit with writer Al Hirshberg and say: "I had satisfied my lifelong ambition. I was with a winner at last."

CHAPTER 10

At Home with Cousy

HE HAD been on the road for ten days, hopping by plane from Philadelphia to Cincinnati to St. Louis to Los Angeles, then back to Minneapolis, then to New York. After the game at Madison Square Garden, he and the other Celtics threw their sweaty uniforms into canvas satchels and rushed to get cabs to take them to the airport.

They landed at Boston's Logan Airport at a little past two o'clock in the morning. Cousy and Heinsohn got into Tom's car (he had parked it at the airport), and the two drove back to their homes in Worcester. It was well after four o'clock before Cousy got to bed.

He slept most of the day, arising about three to get acquainted again with his two daughters, Mary Patricia and Marie Colette, who were just home from grade school.

That evening he drove back to Boston with Heinsohn and their two wives for a game that night at the Garden against the Syracuse Nats. The Nats were leading in the third period when Cousy suddenly exploded for 12 points within six minutes. Boston won, 117-112.

After the game he sat around the dressing room for about an hour, the dark, pointed face grinning as he talked to reporters and greeted old friends.

An usher came into the room and hovered at the edge of the crowd. Cousy saw him. "Something for me?" he asked.

"Well," said the usher, a little hesitantly, "there's a kid outside in a wheelchair with his parents. They wanted to know if you could shake the kid's hand. He's a big fan of yours, but I told them that—"

"Where is he?" said Cousy.

The usher quickly ran to the door and opened it.

A mob of boys and girls stood outside. When they saw their hero, they began yelling "Cooz! Cooz!" thrusting books and sheets of paper at him to sign.

Patiently, poker-faced, saying little, he slowly inched his way through the mob, signing autographs right and left. By the time he finished, he had signed his name 37 times.

Sometime, just for fun, sign your name 37 times. It can be dull work, even tiring; your hand will probably ache when you finish. Then imagine you have to sign it 37 more times, perhaps within the hour, while people are yelling in your ears and tugging at your sleeves. Remember that while all this is going on, you must never seem displeased or annoyed. Otherwise, people will say you have a big head. Remember that you must be willing to sign your name at any time, even while you are sitting in a restaurant just about to knife into a thick, juicy steak. Now you have some idea of what it's like to be a sports idol.

Cousy finally signed all the autographs and made his way to where the boy in the wheelchair was waiting. He leaned over the wheelchair, said hello, and began to talk to the boy. The kid's face looked up at him, shining with admiration; you could see that the boy could hardly believe it—here, right in front of him, was his hero, Bob Cousy.

Cousy talked to the boy and his parents for several minutes, patted the child on the shoulder and scuttled back to the dressing room. He showered and dressed, then joined Missie and the Heinsohns in the hallway. They drove back to Worcester, arriving well after one o'clock in the morning.

By nine A.M. the phone was ringing merrily. A Worcester priest was on the wire, to ask Bob to do some work for a local charity. Though he was still sleepy, Bob listened, then agreed. He had a big breakfast, washed down by nearly a quart of milk. And then it was back to the phone. He talked long-distance with a magazine editor in New York who wanted him to pose for a cover. A Boston newspaperman called to get Bob's reactions to the game the preceding night. Then Joe Sharry phoned to say he'd be over in a few minutes to talk about some legal matters.

Sharry is a Worcester businessman. In 1954, Cousy asked Sharry to help him form some kind of union for the NBA players.

At the time, Cousy had no need for a union. He was the highest paid player on the Celtics. He worked for one of the NBA's finest and most generous owners, Walter Brown. But Cousy knew that other NBA players were being paid poorly. He knew that NBA owners were scheduling exhibition games during the regular season; as a result, some players were near physical collapse after playing as many as six and seven games a week.

The players complained to Cousy. Why didn't they complain to the league president? he asked them. How could they? they said. If their boss found out about it —and of course he would—they'd be fired. But Cousy could complain. Nobody was going to fire the league's biggest star.

On his own time and with his own money, helped by Dolph Schayes and a few others, Cousy began organizing a union. He wrote to players on all the teams, asking them to join the union. Then he went to the NBA president, Maurice Podoloff, and presented him with a list of the players' demands.

Podoloff brushed him off. But from 1954 through 1956, even though most of the other NBA players became discouraged and left Cousy to fight alone, he and Joe Sharry kept up the pressure on Podoloff and the owners. Finally, in 1957, the NBA recognized the union and gave to Cousy and the players most of the reforms they had asked for.

Unfortunately, some NBA owners still look upon the league as a kind of sweatshop operation, with the players being so many pants pressers. The more games they play, the lower the cost per player per game. But by his presence and the rules of the NBA players' union, Cousy kept the greedier ones from scheduling games every night and twice on Sundays.

Missie Cousy was busy making pots of coffee in the kitchen as Bob talked with Joe Sharry in the living room. On the coffee table in front of them were sheets of paper. Bob leafed through them with the acumen of a cost accountant, pointing a pencil to an entry here, asking Sharry a question about an entry there. Some of the papers were concerned with the insurance business that Bob was running in Worcester; others with a restaurant he was thinking about buying.

Bob Cousy is a businessman, make no mistake about that. And a good businessman with a sharp eye for a dollar. Always was. . . .

When Cousy came out of Holy Cross, he was fired up with a dozen ways to make himself a millionaire before he was thirty. He and Frank Oftring opened a gas station, figuring that every Holy Cross fan in New England would want their cars to cruise on Cousy-Oftring gas.

They didn't, and it wasn't long before Cousy sold his interest in the station. But Cousy was undaunted, his get-rich-quick dreams still intact. One summer he and Joe Sharry decided to stage summer basketball games on Cape Cod.

"Thousands and thousands of people come to Cape Cod each summer," he told Sharry. "Lots of them are basketball fans. They'll be delighted to pay a dollar or so to see basketball in the summer."

Cousy recruited some of his old Holy Cross teammates. Sharry billed Bob as THE HOUDINI OF THE HARDWOOD, and arranged for some semipro teams in the area to play against Cousy's "All-Star" team. Cousy and Sharry had done everything to make their venture a success, but they had forgotten one little thing: The wind can blow cold at night on old Cape Cod. And few fans were willing to sit in open stands and freeze—even to see the Houdini of the Hardwood. As a result, Houdini dropped a considerable sum of money.

He made that money back—and more with it—on a number of subsequent business ventures. These included a Worcester insurance business, some restaurants, and his interest in Camp Graylag, his summer camp for boys in Pittsfield, New Hampshire. Each summer several hundred boys attend the camp; Bob is there personally most of the summer, and during two weeks in late August at the camp he directs a basketball instructional clinic.

Like all famous athletes, Cousy gives advertising testimonials for various products, such as sporting goods and a milk company. Other companies have asked Cousy for testimonials, but he has refused because he did not use the product himself or because he would not recommend it to younger people.

All these ventures made Cousy a wealthy man. He was making $40,000 a year from the Celtics during the latter part of his career, and probably at least that much from his other interests. But he was never one to rest on his bank account; he always kept his eyes open for other lucrative business opportunities.

Most everybody likes to make a great deal of money, of course, and Cousy is no exception. He came from a poor family where, if you had one dollar in your pocket, your mind swam as you tried to imagine what you would do with all that money. You think a lot about money if you live in the slums; and when you think enough about a thing, it can become very important to you.

Not that money is the most important thing in Cousy's life. Far from it. Apart from his family, winning is probably the most important thing in Bob Cousy's life. Cousy is always trying to win, whether it's a softball game with some friends, an NBA championship, a union for players, or a profit for one of his businesses. "I," he says, "am a lousy loser."

After Bob had finished talking with Sharry, he had conferences with several lawyers and businessmen about a restaurant he was thinking of buying. As the men talked, Missie kept the cups of coffee coming from the kitchen, though Cousy stuck to his favorite: milk.

After the men left, Bob stretched out on the couch with a current best seller, *Advise and Consent*. He does a great deal of reading—historical novels and books on political subjects. He was a good student at Holy Cross, but he thinks he could have been a better one.

Around 1954 or 1955, he says, "I realized that I got very little out of college. All of a sudden, I had a strong craving for knowledge. I got tired of spending the days watching the television screen or going to the movies.

"I talked to one of my teachers at Holy Cross, Father Pat Haran, and he set up a reading program for me. I have so much time traveling and sitting around hotel rooms that I can put to better use reading.

"This all began when I started to read some best-selling novels. I enjoyed them, but I wanted more. Now Father Haran has me reading things like psychology, history and philosophy. I should have got around to these a long time ago."

As a man who had to travel in the world of business, Cousy realized that he needed to know how to speak correctly. Several years ago he began the practice of going through the dictionary at the beginning of each week and picking out five words that he did not ordinarily use, not fancy-sounding words but words that any college graduate should use. During the next seven days he tried to work the five words into his conversation, so that he would know how to use them comfortably and correctly.

Both Bob and Missie keep active in community work in Worcester: charity drives, school-improvement programs, and so on. And as all good citizens should, they keep up-to-date on current events—in their community and in the nation. Missie, in particular, often dashes off letters to her Congressman, giving her views on political problems. Once she wrote to Harold Stassen, then a government official, giving her opinions on a political crisis in Argentina.

Stassen replied to her letter, thanking her. In the same mail was a letter to Bob with the return address, The White House. Since the White House is a well-known restaurant in Worcester, Missie paid it no mind.

That night, when Bob got home, Missie met him excitedly. "You know who I got a letter from?" she asked.

"Congressman Donahue!" said Cousy, well aware that Missie was always writing to her Congressman.

"Yes, and someone else."

"Who?"

"Harold Stassen."

"Well, I'll be jiggered," said Cousy, surprise in his voice.

He began to go through his mail. He opened the envelope that had the return address, The White House. "Hey, Missie," he shouted, "come here, quick!"

"What's the matter?" she said.

"You get letters from Congressmen? You get letters from Harold Stassen? Look who I got a letter from!"

The letter invited Bob to attend a White House conference on physical fitness. It was signed by President Eisenhower.

After reading for several hours, Cousy went to see his Worcester neighbor, Tom Heinsohn. The Gunner also has an insurance business in Worcester. He and Cousy kid each other about who's taking business away from whom, but both compete as hard for business as they do for basketball victories. As a result, Bob has lost some customers to Tommy, and Tommy has lost some to Bob.

Now they were talking about the restaurant that Cousy and a partner were considering buying. Heinsohn asked if Cousy planned on changing the name of the restaurant.

"We're still undecided," said Bob. "My partner wants to call it Bob Cousy's Abner Wheeler House, but I'm sort of partial to Abner Wheeler's Bob Cousy House. More class."

For a while they talked about Red Auerbach, a Chinese food enthusiast, who had an interest in a Chinese restaurant in Boston. Then the talk drifted to one of Cousy's most recent interests: learning how to play the piano.

"If you're still thinking of taking up the piano," said Heinsohn, grinning, "it might cut down on your overhead at your restaurant. You could be featured in the lounge playing 'Chopsticks.'"

"That's good clear thinking," said Cousy, laughing. "I'll break the act in at Auerbach's place."

In the evening Cousy sat in the living room playing and talking with his two daughters. Marie Colette suddenly turned to him and said, "Daddy, why are you away from home so much?"

"I have to be, sweetie," he said. "You know I have to play basketball with the team."

"But if you were hurt," said Marie, "then you'd have to stay home with us."

"That's right."

"Well," said Marie, "then I hope that in the next game you break a leg."

A cold, icy wind, carrying flakes of snow with it, was blowing outside the window of the Cousy home. Inside, Cousy lolled on a couch, listening contentedly to the music from the hi-fi and watching his daughter do graceful handsprings on the floor.

Then Missie noticed the time: Bob had less than three hours to drive to Boston to catch the Celtics' plane, which was leaving that evening on another long road trip. Cousy got up slowly and then he grinned at Missie.

"I suppose," he said, "that it's a good thing I love my work."

CHAPTER 11

"You Get Used to It"

You are on a road trip with Bob Cousy and the Boston Celtics. The big jet has just taken off from Boston's Logan Airport on a clear, icy January night. As the plane rises steeply into the sky, you turn to the dark-haired man in the seat next to you.

As usual there is a brooding, faraway look on Cousy's long face. If you didn't know him, you might hesitate about breaking into his reverie. But this is Bob Cousy, friendly and easy to talk to, relaxed and articulate. You can talk to him for hours with never a strain in the conversation.

You talk about how basketball has changed since his days at Andrew Jackson. He nods. "There's no doubt about it, John," he says (he never forgets to drop your name often in a conversation). "The biggest change in basketball during the past decade has been the jump shot. I was looking at some films of one of our Holy Cross games recently. Do you know how many jump shots there were in the *entire* game? Just four. Today I'd bet the reverse is true; a college team would take only four long shots that *weren't* jumpers.

"But I do think the shot is way overdone. Once you have left your feet, you have committed yourself. There are only two things you can do—shoot or pass. If you can't do either one because you're guarded too closely, you're a dead duck. When you have both feet on the ground, you can shoot, pass, or dribble around your man.

"Then there's another thing about the jump shot. Too many kids practice the jumper and nothing else. Oh, it might make them big scorers in high school or college. But up here in the NBA, you have to be able to do something else besides shoot with a jumper from thirty feet out. When teams find out that you have only one shot, they adjust their defenses and bottle you up. That's why so many All-Americans are busts in the NBA. They have just one shot. You need a wide repertoire of shots."

One of the Celtics comes up the aisle. He wants Cousy to join him in a card game at the other end of the cabin. "We like Bob to play," says the player, grinning, "because he's the only one who can figure out the score at the end."

At two in the morning the jet lands at the Cincinnati airport. Hunching up their shoulders against the wind, the players walk to a bus, carrying their suitcases. The bus takes them to downtown Cincinnati. It's close to three o'clock as they walk through the hushed lobby, their shoes clacking on the marble floor. Cousy picks up his room key, looks regretfully at the sign that says CLOSED on the coffee shop door, then walks slowly to the elevator.

The team comes down for what might be called breakfast at around 12:30 the next afternoon. Cousy walks through the lobby in the somnolent way he has. He sits at a small table in the coffee shop with Tommy Heinsohn and orders a huge slab of roast beef, two glasses of milk, and a gigantic piece of ice cream.

Some of the players are going to a movie down the street. "Cooz," asks Frank Ramsey, "want to come along? It's an all-horror show."

"No thanks," says Cousy. "I think I'll read a little."

Up in his room he flops on his bed and opens a book to a page mark. The book is *Total Empire,* by Edmund A. Walsh, S. J. It details the Communist plan to control the world. "Mostly I don't read books as heavy as this," Cousy tells you. "Like in the past year I've read things like *To Kill a Mockingbird, The Making of a President, The Devil's Advocate.* But at least I've graduated from Mickey Spillane."

He looks out the window. "I'll tell you frankly," he says, "it amazes me how some athletes never try to improve themselves. You've got to remember that one day you're not going to be an athlete, and you have to be prepared for that day."

He thinks for a moment about those athletes who do not work to improve themselves. "You'd think," he says, "that college men would have more sense."

He laughs. "But don't get the idea that I'm an intellectual or any Big Brain. I just want to be able to hold my own."

That evening the Celtics assemble in the hotel lobby. People stop to stare at the clump of tall men and the one fellow in the middle who seems so much shorter. If this is a basketball team, that little guy must be the water boy.

In the taxi on the way to the arena, the water boy and the coach talk about how they will play the Royals that night.

"Well, Arnold," says Cousy, "I think that . . ."

Sitting in the front seat, you listen. It seems strange to hear Auerbach being called Arnold; most everybody calls him Red, but to Cousy he is always Arnold.

The two are very close. Once, in fact, Auerbach commented: "I never have said anything publicly about this, but often when we'd have a new man on the club, I'd ask Cousy what he thought of him. Out there on the court, Bob could often tell better than anybody how well the new man was fitting into our pattern."

Auerbach thought for a moment. "Of course," he said, "there's a real line between a coach and his players. A coach can't play cards, share a room, or socialize with his players if he expects to be a success.

"Now, Cousy never deliberately crossed this line. It just happened. We share a lot of the same views about pro basketball, and for this reason I have taken Bob into my confidence on more than a few occasions.

"He and I have also made three trips overseas for the U. S. State Department [giving basketball instruction in various countries]. We were together constantly on those trips and as a result we got to know each other extremely well. But Cousy has never taken advantage of my friendship, nor have I of his."

At the Cincinnati arena, the Celtics put on their uniforms in a little room under the stands, loudly swapping wisecracks and insults. "They're a good bunch," Cousy once said to writer Irv Goodman. "We have no troubles, no jealousies. With the shooters we have, I feel I don't have to shoot too much. I don't worry about my scoring average. I know we'll get the points. I figure I can do more good getting the ball in to them. It's part of the way we are on this team, but it's become almost automatic with me, to get my passes in to the other fellows.

"If I've been working one side of the court too steady, without consciously thinking about it I move to the other side to give the other fellows a chance. Not that anyone ever complains about not seeing the ball enough. That doesn't happen. But it is a part of the way we feel that we want everybody to share in the game."

Now the Celtics are coming out onto the court, led by their captain with the big number 14 on his back. Once Bill Sharman was telling some friends what it was like to follow the Cooz onto a court:

"I can never remember a single time," he said, "when he did any one thing which would make him a leader in the dressing room. No phony speeches. No big talks. It was just that when you went out on the floor, there he was and things had to get better. In the clutch, he would take everybody on his shoulders and carry them."

Cousy plays all of the first quarter, half of the second. Midway through the third period he comes back into the game with the Celtics trailing by three points. Watching from the press box, you can see the Celtics suddenly seem to spring alive, like a tired runner getting a whiff of oxygen. Ernie Barrett, a former Celtic, once put it this way: "Cooz keeps that ball moving and he keeps the fellows moving. He gives this club a lift just being out there. He doesn't stop and look around and wonder what to do. Whatever the club needs done, he does. The fellows know it. It's quite a feeling."

Out on the court Cousy has just thrown in a long, looping one-hander. He feeds Russell in the bucket for another two points and suddenly the Celtics are off on a scoring splurge that nets them 18 points within the next six minutes.

Now the Celtics lead by 13, but late in the game Oscar Robertson and the Royals rally and the Celtic lead is cut to three. With seconds remaining, the Cooz has the ball. He dribbles out the clock, pursued by three frantic Royals, and the Celtics go off the winners.

Someone once asked Red Auerbach why Cousy was such a great dribbler. "His long arms, quick reflexes, and flexible wrists enable him to do things in a game I never thought possible," said Auerbach. "Because of his shoulders, wrists and hands, Cousy can dribble from the front, from either side, or from the back, without breaking his stride, twisting his body, or changing cadence of his dribble. I've never before seen a basketball player who could do that. Everyone else has to tip off his intention somehow."

In the dressing room after the game, Cousy shouts, "Good game, gang," as he heads for the showers.

"That's what we look for," Auerbach is telling a reporter; "that hot streak and then we go."

"Yeah," someone else says, "and you know who strikes the match to get them hot—the Cooz. Look it up sometime, and see how he gets most of his points when the pressure's on, when they count."

It's near midnight when you and the Celtics take off on a chartered DC-3 for the flight to St. Louis. Cousy gets into a game of cards with Heinsohn and several sportswriters.

"What are you playing?" someone asks.

"Aw, Hell."

"I'm sorry I asked," says the kibitzer, offended.

"No, you don't understand," says Cousy. "That's the name of the game—Aw, Hell."

The game is a form of bridge, but terribly complicated. The kibitzer sees quickly that only Cousy and Heinsohn seem to know how to keep score. Perhaps not so coincidentally, Cousy seems to be winning.

The plane lands at dawn in St. Louis. Some of the players have slept, but most—like Cousy—have read or played cards. The wind is cold and cutting as they come off the plane, but Cousy stands at the bottom of the ramp, holding all the other cardplayers around him until he makes a final accounting.

"I win twenty-five cents," he says. Solemnly, the others pay him.

"You mean you sat up all night playing for twenty-five cents?" says the kibitzer.

"Better than losing twenty-five cents," says Cousy.

They arrive at their hotel at 7:30. "Put in a call for twelve," Auerbach yells. They have a game with the Hawks at two o'clock that afternoon.

At 11:30 Cousy rouses himself from bed, shaves, and has a quick breakfast. By 12:30 he is on his way to Kiel Auditorium for the game with the Hawks.

The Celtics lose, and for a while after the game, Cousy sits alone, head bowed and hands clasped. A friend tries to cheer him up. "How could you expect to win with only four hours' sleep," says the friend.

"Look," says Cousy, staring solemnly at the ground. "I never go into a game expecting we're going to lose."

Later, after a thick roast-beef dinner, someone suggests a movie. It is after seven when they go into the theatre, past ten when they leave.

"Some cards?" suggests Heinsohn.

"No," says Cousy, "I think I'll sit up and read for a while."

He finally goes to bed at 4. He is up by 12. On one Celtic road trip, writer Al Hirshberg tagged along after Cousy for *Sport* magazine. Hirshberg asked Cousy why he didn't go to bed earlier on an off-day. "There's no sense in my going to bed early," explained Cousy. "I just toss round half the night and then get up exhausted."

But how could he play with only four hours' sleep?

"My legs," said Cousy, "they're my strongest asset. The bulk of my weight is below my waist. I look about 160, but I weigh around 185. Nobody ever believes that until they see me standing on the scales."

"This guy can run forever," said Sharman.

"I grew up playing basketball on concrete outdoor courts on Long Island," added Cousy. "I never played indoors as a kid. I built up my legs on those hard courts, and when it came time to play on wooden floors, it was that much easier for me."

The next day is also an off-day. Nevertheless, most of the Celtics stay in bed until about noon, have a late breakfast and lounge around the hotel lobby. Cousy and Sharman spend most of the day reading; after supper, they go to a movie, return about 10 and play cards till after 1.

Why, asked Hirshberg, didn't they get up early and spend a normal day when they didn't have a game to play?

"Because it would throw our schedule all out of kilter," answered Cousy. "We play most of our games at night, so we gear our lives accordingly. We eat a big meal around three in the afternoon, then take in a movie or loaf around the room and go to the arena about an hour or so before a game. Then we eat again after it's over and get to bed at one-thirty or two in the morning.

"But on our days off, we have to do the same thing because we don't have enough days off to shift to a normal routine."

Willie Sharman, who had played baseball in the

Dodger chain, was listening. "You know how baseball players hate to go from day games to night games and back again," he said. "Well, we're the same way except we play more nights than ballplayers do. The worst thing for us is a day game, because that messes everything up."

The next morning the Celtics fly out of St. Louis for a game that evening in Syracuse. After the game—they won—the Celtics go directly to the airport, from where they are to fly to Philadelphia. There is a delay getting on the chartered plane, because the writers who travel with the Celtics are back at the arena finishing their stories and putting them on the wires to Boston. Impatient and tired, one of the Celtic players snarls that the blinking writers are always late.

"Never squawk when the writers are working," says Cousy in a voice that's soft even when he's angry. "If you're lucky, they may be writing about you."

"They might be beating my brains out, too," says the player.

Cousy laughs. "I'd rather have them beat my brains out than not mention me at all."

"There are athletes," says someone, "who don't have much use for writers."

"I feel sorry for them," says Cousy. "They don't realize how much help writers can give them. I don't know where we'd be without the writers. Basketball is over fifty years old, but the game never really caught on until the writers began telling the world about it."

He pauses, thinking about something. "You know," he says, looking out at the lights of the airport runway, "there are some people who think they're more important than anyone else just because they have some God-given talent—maybe they're athletes, maybe artists, maybe stage and screen people, maybe even writers. But I'll tell you this, no matter how big a person is, there's never an excuse for his having a big head."

The next night the Celtics play in Philadelphia, go on to New York for another game, then back to Philadelphia, then another game in Syracuse before returning home after being on the road for 11 days and seven games.

It has been 11 days of rushing to airports, checking into hotels at dawn, eating breakfasts at twelve and dinners at one in the morning, running to arenas, and playing 48 minutes of hard-driving basketball.

Once, after a long trip, the Celtics arrived back at Logan Airport. As they were walking to their cars, one of the rookies suddenly doubled over, stricken by stomach cramps. Cousy looked at him sympathetically. "It's the irregular living," he said. "He'll get used to it."

CHAPTER 12

The Champs No Longer

THE 1957-58 season began for the newly crowned champions with a bang. It ended with a thud.

During the first month of the season, the Celtics were the terror of the league, jumping into first place from the opening whistle and building a bigger and bigger lead. Willie Sharman was leading the scoring, averaging 22 points a game, and Cousy was next with 18, one of the few times in NBA history when the two backcourtmen were a club's leading scorers.

Helping out were Tommy Heinsohn, in his second year, who was sinking 17 a game, and Bill Russell and Frank Ramsey, who were averaging 16. It was a finely balanced team, with even the men on the bench—Lou Tsioropoulos, Jack Nichols, Arnie Risen, Sam Jones and Andy Phillip—capable of pitching in 20 or 30 points on a night when one of the regulars was injured.

The race looked like a Celtic runaway; the other

teams battled to stop them—one way or the other. In a game against Philadelphia, Cousy and big Neil Johnston collided. Cousy's knee was badly injured. After the game, Cousy angrily told a newspaperman that Johnston had kneed him deliberately.

The next day's headlines were black and bold:

COUSY RAPS JOHNSTON, CHARGES "DELIBERATE FOUL"

Some athletes, awakening the next morning calmer and cooler, would have ducked the controversy—and an angry Johnston—by claiming they had been misquoted. Of course, this would reflect on some innocent reporter's reputation for accuracy, but the reputation of reporters is a matter that concerns few pro athletes.

Cousy awoke calmer and cooler, well aware that he should not have made such a charge in public, no matter what he thought privately. If you are a pro athlete, you are not supposed to go around accusing other players of dirty pool. It is not good for your relationship with other players, and it is not good for the game in which you are making a living.

Cousy knew well that he could get out of the jam simply by saying he had been misquoted. Cousy said he had been quoted correctly.

"After being around seven or eight years," he later told Irv Goodman of *Sport*, "I should have known better than to shoot off my mouth. I didn't mean that Johnston played dirty or that he goes out of his way to hurt you. But that knee in my thigh, that one act, I felt was deliberate. It's happened to me seven or eight times, always by bigger fellows who, instead of taking their normal defensive position and playing me, have hit me as I went by.

"I didn't plan to accuse Johnston. Five writers called me about the injury, and only the last one asked if I thought it was deliberate. And I told him, yes, I thought it was deliberate. I've explained all this to Johnston, and things are okay between us. . . . I still feel the bang was deliberate—a way to stop me from driving by. I just shouldn't have said so."

Others were banging Cousy as he drove by. The Celtics retaliated but they missed their big "policeman," Jungle Jim Loscutoff, who was out nearly all of the season with a bad knee. Of course they did have big Arnie Risen and Jack Nichols, but no one was more respected around the league than Loscutoff.

Once Knick Coach Vince Boryla charged that Red Auerbach had ordered Loscutoff to rough up his star, lean Kenny Sears. A short while later, the Celtics arrived in New York for a game. In a hotel lobby, Loscutoff spotted Boryla, a huge man himself—6-foot-4 and well over 200 pounds. Loscutoff walked up to Boryla, and said in a hard, quiet voice: "Why'd you say that, Vince? That's the way I play. Maybe it's hard, but it's my style. What am I supposed to do, let Sears run over me?"

Boryla said nothing.

The Celtics did not endear themselves to the rest of the league. During a game, the fiery Auerbach would rant and rave at referees, call them "blind Toms" and stronger names. And midway through the fourth period, when the Celtics had built up a safe lead, he'd whip out a fat cigar and light it, then lean back and savor the aroma—a tactic well calculated to madden the opposing coach and hometown fans.

There were those who claimed that Auerbach would do anything to win a game, even send out a hatchet-man to injure an opposing player who had suddenly got hot. "This isn't a namby-pamby game," snapped the crusty Auerbach when he heard that kind of talk, "but I'd never, never order somebody to hurt another player. I want to win, but I want to win clean."

But whatever emotions the Celtics aroused in fans around the league, they had no trouble winning the Eastern Division title, winning 44 and losing 28, finishing a whopping six games ahead of second-place Philadelphia.

Philadelphia beat Syracuse in the best-of-three opening play-offs, and now these two old foes—Neil Johnston's Warriors and Bob Cousy's Celtics—met in the play-off to decide the Eastern champion. It was a bitter battle, Boston finally winning 93-88, in the fifth and final game.

In the West the St. Louis Hawks had finished first in the regular season. This was a powerhouse, with Pettit and Hagan and Macauley the scoring stars and big Charley Share—the man the Celtics once picked in the draft over Cousy—doing the rebounding. And in the backcourt was that old nemesis of Cousy's—Dugie Martin.

Like the Celtics in the East, the Hawks were extended—by Detroit—through five games before winning the western championship. On March 29, the two tired teams lined up to face each other at the Boston Garden in the first game of the best-of-seven series.

A capacity crowd was again on hand to cheer every Celtic basket. But the crowd left subdued; with Pettit hot and with Martin putting handcuffs on Cousy, the Hawks won, 104-102.

The Celtics bounced back to win the next game, 136-112. The two teams went off to St. Louis, where Boston would lose much more than the third game.

In the third period of the game, Bill Russell snaked high into the air to pull down a rebound. He came down awkwardly, landing heavily on one foot; the leg collapsed under him and he crashed to the floor.

Trainer Buddy LeRoux and Auerbach rushed out onto the court. Russell tried to stand; then, holding someone's shoulder, he gingerly put his weight down on the injured ankle. His face contorted with sudden pain.

A low, excited buzz ran through Kiel Auditorium as the big guy was helped off the floor, limping badly on the ankle. The partisan crowd knew well how much the Celtics needed Russell; without him, the Celtics could not get the ball often enough for their patented fast break. St. Louis came on to win the third game, 111-107.

Down two games to one, the Celtics had to play the fourth game without Russell. Big Arnie Risen and Jack Nichols filled in for him, but neither could get the number of rebounds that Russell was capable of grabbing. However, Auerbach and Cousy had an idea, an idea that they showed to the Hawks near the end of the fourth game.

The 5-foot-10 Dugie Martin was covering Cousy as tightly as usual, running and cutting eyeball-to-eyeball with him. But midway through the final period, Cousy suddenly cut under the basket into the pivot man's position—and stopped.

The crowd let out a sudden, surprised roar. Cousy was taking Martin into the bucket. The smallest guy on the Boston team was playing the pivot.

But Cousy had three inches on Martin. If Martin tried to play between Cousy and the ball, Cousy could leap high to grab a pass and score. If Martin stayed behind Cousy—between Bob and the basket—Cousy could grab a quick pass, then wheel like a pivot man for a hook shot.

The St. Louis crowd began to laugh at this strange sight, these two small men playing in the bucket—where giants usually wheel and hook. They were like children playing the parts of grown men. But then the Hawks' fans stopped laughing, for Bob Cousy was playing this part as though he had played it all his life.

He spun. Two points. Another pass, another hook, another two points. He scored seven quick points before the Hawks rushed in a bigger man to guard him, and the seven were enough to break open a tight game. The Celtics won, 109-98, and now the two teams were tied at two games apiece.

Back in Boston for the fifth game, Cousy knew the trick wouldn't work a second time. While trainers worked on Russell's sprained ankle, the Celtics tried to develop a new attack, one depending less on the fast break. But by the fourth period of the fifth game, the Hawks had a fat lead.

Then Cousy, as he had done so often in the past, began to rally the Celtics. He scored eight points in the final few minutes, but the last-gasp effort just fell short. The Hawks held on to win, 102-100, and lead three games to two.

The Celtics knew what had to be done: Somehow Russell had to be able to play if the Celtics were to retain their championship. Gallantly, the big fellow limped out onto the court at Kiel Auditorium for the start of the sixth game.

During the first few minutes, Russell seemed to be soaring as high as ever, plucking rebounds off the boards like so many apples off a tree. First the Hawks were ahead, then the Celtics, but in the third period— with Russell out to rest his ankle—the Hawks inched ahead.

Midway through the fourth period, Russell came back into the game, limping badly now. It was a last, climactic effort, and for a little while it seemed to be enough. Cousy scored a basket, his fifteenth point of the night, and the Celtics were ahead.

But Bob Pettit came loping downcourt for the Hawks, unleashing long jump shots that seemed to run on guide wires into the basket. With 11 seconds to go, he hit on a long jumper and the Hawks were ahead, 110-107.

Sharman stormed upcourt for the Celtics and threw

in a one-hander. *St. Louis 110, Boston 109.* The auditorium was a bedlam of sound as the Hawks brought the ball down cautiously. "Freeze it! freeze it!" screamed the fans, who had poured down onto the side of the court.

The Hawks gave the ball to little Dugie Martin. Cousy pounced on him, but Martin dribbled away, and now the Cooz—so often the dribbler running out the clock—was the pursuer as the clock began to run out on him.

He dived at that bouncing ball, open air between him and the basket, but Martin bounced the ball away. Cousy wheeled to give chase, the long hands swiping at that elusive ball, grasping for it. . . .

A Niagara of sound flowed down onto the court as these two zigged and zagged, like two weird dancers, and then—sawing through the noise—came the final buzzer.

The Hawk fans spilled onto the floor; they grabbed Martin and Pettit, hoisted them high on bobbing shoulders. His head down, Cousy pushed his way through the crowd toward the dressing room. . . .

The Celtics sat quietly in their dressing room for a long time, the defeated champions, looking at each other, shaking their heads, not trusting their voices to speak. But once in a while the quiet was broken by dry, retching sobs that came from one corner of the room where Cousy sat alone. One by one his teammates came by, patting him on the shoulder, but he kept his head down, the shoulders heaving.

It wasn't that he had scored only 15 points or that the Celtics had lost. Inwardly, as Cousy explained months later, he was cursing himself because he felt he had failed his team. Before the game, somehow, he had not been able to build up that full-blown storm of rage. He had gone out on the floor lacking that Cousy killer instinct to win. He had failed this team, this team that he led, and he could not find forgiveness for himself.

But over the months, Cousy found something else to replace forgiveness: He promised himself that never again would he go out onto a court for a big game without that need to win boiling inside him. It was a promise that would eventually do what nothing else in basketball had ever done. It would stop the Cooz.

The following season, 1958-59, the Celtics romped home first in the Eastern Division by an even bigger margin than the previous year. They won 52, lost only 20, and finished a ridiculous 12 games ahead of second-place New York. Again Cousy led the league in assists, Russell was the leader in rebounds, and Sharman, Cousy and Heinsohn were bunched among the top 15 scorers, each averaging around 15 points a game.

But the eyes of the Celtics were on one goal all season long: the NBA championship. If Russell had not been hurt in the 1957-58 play-off, the championship trophy would now be sitting in the Boston Garden. Everybody in Boston said so. Now the Celtics would go out and prove it.

Then came Syracuse and near-disaster.

Syracuse had beaten the Knickerbockers in the opening Eastern Division play-offs. With their big star, Dolph Schayes, red-hot, they barged into Boston almost trembling with eagerness to destroy the Celtics.

Boston won the first game and Syracuse the second, and so the best-of-seven series swayed, each team winning in turn, until they were tied—three games apiece —with the seventh and final game to be played at Boston Garden.

That was the game in which the Nats led by 17 points at the half, the game in which angry Boston fans shouted "choke-up artists" at the Celtics, the game in which the Cooz—gasping for breath and collapsing during time outs—led a frantic comeback charge that caught the Nats and beat them, 130-125.

It was after that game that Cousy sat, his body shaking, on a dressing room table for a long 45 minutes, while teammates came by and silently patted him on the back. It was after that game that Cousy turned to a reporter and said, "Well, we showed 'em we aren't choke-up artists, didn't we? We showed 'em, huh?"

And perhaps it was after that game that Cousy found self-forgiveness for what he considered his failure in the game the previous season against St. Louis.

The Minneapolis Lakers had dethroned the Hawks as Western champions. The Lakers were a young and exciting team, led by an amazing 6-foot-5 rookie—Elgin Baylor—who had averaged an astounding 25 points a game in his first NBA season. It was a tough, gutsy team; down three games to two in the Western play-off against the Hawks, it had bounced back to win the final two games, 98-97 and 106-104.

The Celtics looked tired after their exhausting series against Syracuse. The younger Laker team looked confident, its rough edges scalded off in the pressure-cooking series against St. Louis.

But as the best-of-seven series began, you could see the Celtics throwing off their fatigue. The Cooz had them running, and they ran right past the bewildered young Lakers in the first game, winning 118-115. Boston was still running the next night, winning 128-108. The two teams went to Minneapolis-St. Paul for the third game. Reported The Associated Press: "With Bob Cousy engineering the fast break and Bill Russell a mainstay of the defense, the Celtics took command late in the first quarter and never were in jeopardy after that." The Celtics won, 123-120, with Cousy scoring 23.

Two days later the Celtics made it four in a row—the first time it had ever been done in NBA history—by winning, 118-113.

In the Celtics' dressing room, they yelled and poured beer over Cousy. He sat with his back to a wall, a creased grin on his face, a look of satisfaction in his eyes. The NBA championship was going back to where it belonged—in Boston—and as long as Bob Cousy was a Celtic, it would stay there.

CHAPTER 13

"Better Be Your Best, Bob"

"FOR years everybody has been waiting for the new Cousy, but there's no need to wait any longer. The Big O has replaced the Big C."

Bob Cousy read those words carefully. They were in a column written by New York *Post* columnist Milton Gross halfway through the 1960-61 season. In the column, Gross was comparing Cousy to Oscar "Big O" Robertson, an All-American playing his first year with the Cincinnati Royals. Someone had clipped out the column and mailed it to Cousy.

Bob read what Gross had written:

> Cousy had and still has considerably more flash than Oscar and probably better hands. But there seems to be growing sentiment in the league, even among those who once would give Robertson no more than grudging admiration, that the rookie is the equal or better than Bob in about every other phase of the game.

Without question Oscar is the better shooter, a far better and more useful defensive player, of infinitely more value and effectiveness as a rebounder, and his equal as a feeder. There may be some disagreement in some quarters on this last, but the disagreement would come principally because Cousy's pass is made with a flourish.

Gross compared the current statistics. Robertson was averaging 31 points a game and leading the league in assists. Cousy was averaging 18; he was second to Robertson in assists.

Then Gross turned to the 1960-61 East-West All-Star game, played a few weeks earlier. Both had played in the backcourt for the East. Cousy had scored a measly four points. The Big O had scored 23 and was voted the game's Most Valuable Player.

A few weeks after Gross' column was published, the Celtics came to Madison Square Garden for a game against the Knickerbockers. After that game, another New York *Post* writer sat down at his typewriter and wrote that Cousy had displayed "possibly the most artistic three minutes of his basketball life."

He had come into the game midway through the third period with the Knickerbockers ahead, 69-67. He drove past rookie Bobby McNeill and threw in a hook shot. He drove again off the key and sank a fantastic hook from 20 feet away. McNeill fouled him and he sank the two foul shots.

McNeill dropped back and Bob quickly threw in three consecutive one-handed bombs, the last one from a long 35 feet away.

The Knicks dropped a second man off on him. He hit Heinsohn with a quick pass and Heinsohn scored. He threw another pass to Heinsohn and The Gunner hit again.

Moments later the Knicks took a shot and missed. Russell swept the ball off the boards, spun and threw a long pass to Cousy who was racing downcourt. But the pass was overthrown and headed out-of-bounds.

Yet somehow Cousy raced under it and then—leaping with his back to the court—he ticked the ball with one hand, like a tennis player hitting a ball with his back to the net. The ball flew on a line directly into the hands of the Celtics' Sam Jones, who drove all alone for the basket.

Jones missed the easy lay-up (he too may have been startled to find the ball in his hands), but hardly anyone noticed. The big New York crowd was on its feet, stamping, whistling, applauding the Cooz. A little later he came out of the game, his work done, the Celtics ahead by 16.

After the game, a throng of writers gathered around Cousy as he sat on a long green bench in the dressing room. The smiling face glistened with sweat as he looked up at the reporters. Someone asked if he'd been up especially for this game.

"Yes," he said, "this one meant a lot to me. Some guy in this town wrote a column recently comparing me to Oscar Robertson. And I didn't like the way he made the comparison. I really wanted to give a performance in this game, here, in this town."

The reporters asked him about Robertson. "Fantastic ability," he said. "But he must improve in certain departments. Because of the tremendous success he already has achieved, Oscar may forget about trying to improve, and this could hurt him. I read where he says he comes downcourt, looking 80 percent for his shot and 20 percent for play. He has to make it at least a 50-50 proposition."

One of the writers asked if he had thought about quitting. "Well," he said, "I have attained every goal that I can think of. And every year I get to the point where I can't get 'up' for a game. I have to search for things to get me going, like waiting for someone to sock me."

He smiled. "Or someone to write a newspaper column."

He began to unlace his sneakers. "I look for anything which will set off the spark. In past years there were things like my rivalry with Dugie Martin, or playing in Madison Square Garden. But it has become harder and harder to find the spark. I find myself playing three or four bad games in a row.

"Like I say, the hard part is getting yourself 'up.' It's a matter of desire."

He paused, perhaps thinking of the championship game against St. Louis when he felt he hadn't been up. And the promise that he had made. "When the desire's gone," he said, "you have to quit."

He began to laugh. "But I'll tell you," he said, "sometimes my desire overrides my good sense. I think

I hustled too much out there tonight, if there is such a thing as hustling too much. I was really puffing a couple of times."

The pro game had sped up tremendously in the decade that Cousy had been playing. First there had been the 24-second rule, which requires that a team must shoot within that time or lose the ball. Then the league added the bonus-foul rule, which gives an extra free throw on every foul over six that a team commits in a quarter.

"Up until those rules went in," Cousy was saying one day as he lounged in a hotel lobby, "we had so much fouling and stalling, especially near the end of a close game, that the fans got disgusted."

I once asked Cousy if he would suggest any other rule changes to the NBA. "No," he said, laughing, "the owners don't listen to me anyway. I would like to see something done about improving the defense in the league, but to do that you would have to shorten the schedule."

How, I asked, would a shorter schedule help the defense?

"Well, people are always saying that we don't play defense in the NBA. That's a lot of garbage. There's no better defense anywhere. But the only trouble is, we don't have a *sustained* defense, one that's pressing for the entire forty-eight minutes of a game. And that's impossible when you're playing eighty or so games a season. Cut down on the length of the schedule and the quality of the defense would improve."

Critics were loud in panning NBA defense during the late 1950's and early 1960's as a slew of hotshot new scoring stars came into the league. Some were towering seven-footers like Philadelphia's Wilt "the Stilt" Chamberlain. Others, like Oscar Robertson, Jerry West and Elgin Baylor, had unerring one-handed jump shots and a blinding assortment of moves that could literally fake a defender off his feet. In the early Fifties, men like George Mikan had dominated the league by averaging around 25 points a game. In his first year in the league, Chamberlain was averaging 40. Baylor scored 71 in a single game, and later Chamberlain would top that, sinking 100.

But Chamberlain, a moody man, wasn't too happy during his first year in the NBA. He thought the opposition had put too much pressure on him. As usual, the articulate Bob Cousy was asked to be the spokesman for the other NBA players.

"He objects to being double-teamed?" asked Bob. "I've almost always had two men on me. If you're a top man, you have to earn your money. It's part of the business. I feel it's tougher to stay on top than to get on top. Pitchers don't throw at the heads of .220 hitters, do they? How easy does Wilt want it?"

He backed up his words by taking some of the attention away from the new superstars. The first time that the two giants—7-foot Chamberlain and 6-foot-11 Bill Russell—faced each other, the Boston Garden was jammed. Newspapermen from all over the country were on hand to describe this clash of titans. A typical report came from a *Sports Illustrated* writer:

For the 14,000 present at the Garden, the occasion was turned into a double feature by Boston's Bob Cousy, who evidently had not been told what the big attraction was supposed to be. In any event, he dominated the game as he has so often done in recent years—though without adequate recognition, simply because we have all come to take this incredible athlete for granted. Last Saturday, after nine years as a professional, Cousy displayed a dozen sleight-of-hand tricks with the basketball that no one had ever seen before. He set up his teammates for scores all night and made 24 points.

"The hardest thing about playing against Cousy," the veteran Slater Martin has said, "is to resist the temptation to stand around and watch him." From the stands, happily, no one is obliged to resist the temptation. Boston won, 115-106.

Cousy also rose to meet the challenge of the Big O. Though 6-foot-5, four inches taller than Bob, Robertson was a backcourtman like Cousy; inevitably writers like Milton Gross were comparing the two. When the Big O first came to Boston with the Cincinnati team in the early part of the 1960-61 season, Boston writers wrote that Robertson was the new "big small man."

Before the game, Cousy sat in front of his locker, the usual frown on his face, building up a storm inside himself. "It was pride," Cousy said later. "I'd thought about it all week long and talked to myself about it. 'Better get yourself up, Bob. Better be at your best, Bob. Oscar's coming to play in *your* arena, before *your* crowd. . . .' "

Cousy scored first. Robertson came right back with a basket, and so they battled all night. But at the final buzzer it was the "old man" who was a little bit ahead. Cousy scored 27 to Robertson's 25 and Bob outrebounded the bigger man, 7 to 6.

Despite the rise of the new superstars, the Celtics continued to dominate the league. In the 1959-60 season, they won 59 games—tops for any team in NBA history. They beat Philadelphia and big Wilt in the play-offs for the Eastern title, then took on an old foe —the St. Louis Hawks. Again the play-offs came down to a decisive seventh game.

Before the game, Cousy sat in the dressing room, head down, his hands clasped between his bony knees. "Here we go again," he said, building up a rage this time at the NBA system. "One more game. We won more games than any team in the history of the league. And still we're not champions."

Cousy carried his rage onto the court, where he began to hit with long shots. Under the boards he was springing high among the giants to snare rebounds. "He looked," wrote one reporter, "like a small boy climbing a trellis." He scored 19 points, assisted in the scoring of 28 others, enough for an easy 122-103 triumph.

The Celtics had won their second straight championship, their third in four years.

As the 1960-61 season got underway, this was how the Celtics lined up. Willie Sharman and Bob Cousy were still in the backcourt, but the two old pros were now playing two-thirds of most games. Giving them longer and longer breathers were Sam Jones and K. C. Jones, two whippet-fast youngsters. Bill Russell at center was improving his scoring while maintaining his control of the backboards. His sub was long, lean Gene Conley.

At the corners were Tommy Heinsohn and Tom Sanders, a rookie from NYU, with Frank Ramsey still the all-around utility man. The other reserves were Jungle Jim Loscutoff and Gene Guarila.

The Celtics finished first in the 1960-61 Eastern Division race, 11 games ahead of Philadelphia. They beat Syracuse in the Eastern play-offs, then overwhelmed the Hawks in five games to win their third straight NBA championship.

One cold January night in 1962, Bob Cousy returned home to Worcester after a long road trip. His right wrist ached from a sprain and he was limping. He had a Charley horse in his left thigh.

He and Missie sat up talking for a while, and then Bob turned to her and said: "How would you feel about me retiring at the end of the season?"

"I would like to have you quit," said Missie.

"I'm going to think about it seriously when I've got time enough to consider it clearly," said Bob.

Later, talking with the New York *Post*'s Milton Gross (whom he had presumably forgiven for the Big O column), Bob described his feelings about quitting.

"Before this I've never even considered the thought of quitting," he said, "and now I am."

He was considering a full-time career in public relations, creating goodwill work for various companies, said Cousy. After the season ended, the Gillette Razor Company was sending him to France with his family for a tour. He would give lectures on basketball while making friends in France for Gillette. He was also going to Japan for the Jantzen sportswear company.

After he returned, said Cousy, "I'll sit down with the representatives of these two firms and B. F. Goodrich and Seamless Rubber Company, and see what plans they have for me. Gillette is new with me, but all four firms have told me they'd want me with them on a permanent full-time basis. The time has come for me to decide how much of a cut in income I'll have to take. Out of basketball I'll have the advantage of being able to be at home with my family.

"I look at the kids. They're growing up and I haven't done anything with them. I just haven't been home. Maybe it's time I was."

Was he beginning to feel his age—thirty-three? "I don't feel that my reflexes have slowed perceptibly or that I've slowed down so much," Bob told Gross. "Physically I believe I could play another two or three years playing 30, 32, 35 minutes a game, without hurting my play too much."

But Bob admitted that he was bothered by injuries: an aching elbow, a pulled ligament in a knee, the Charley horse, and a pulled muscle in the stomach. "I've had to put hot towels on my stomach before every game," he said. "I've also had a sprained right wrist for three weeks that I've been hitting and hurting again every game. I also twisted my left knee in St. Louis. None of it is serious. It's been one minor thing after another. The trainer tells me it's not age, just bad luck, but all of it has been contributing to my state of mind.

"This is number 12, a long 12, and it seems longer at this time of the year. . . . You wake up and say, 'Who needs it?' It's a matter of putting first things first. Some guys struggling along don't have any choice, but if you're fortunate enough to have other opportunities, you start realizing there are more important things in life. All these things are going around in my mind and I know I can't think them out straight now, but the time's coming when I'll have to sit down and consider everything."

Cousy quit basketball? This game he loved so much? It seemed incredible, even to Cousy. And though he had now talked publicly of quitting—for the first time—he couldn't bring himself to make the move that would end his basketball career: going to Walter Brown and announcing his retirement.

In the 1961-62 season, the Celtics again finished first. And again they won the Eastern championship, beating Philadelphia and Wilt the Stilt. Now they were out to win their fourth straight NBA championship, breaking the record of three straight set by the Minneapolis Lakers in the early 1950's.

Out to stop them from making it four straight were the Lakers, now the Los Angeles Lakers. On the Laker team were two of the greatest of the new superstars: Elgin Baylor and Jerry West, who often combined to score 70 or more points in a single game.

The Lakers and the Celtics split the first six games. And again the Boston Garden was filled as the Celtics trotted out onto the court for another seventh and decisive NBA "World Series."

The two teams were tied 100-100 at the end of four periods; the Lakers' Frank Selvy just missed a lay-up as the buzzer sounded. In the overtime, Baylor hit on two free throws, but Russell and Sam Jones put the Celtics ahead. With two minutes to go in the overtime, Baylor committed his sixth foul and had to leave the game.

He had scored 41 points, tops for both teams. The huge Boston crowd rose to its feet and applauded as this great young scorer came to the sideline, his head down, his breath coming in heaves. The Celtics, too, paid their respects to greatness as their captain, Bob Cousy, ran over and shook Baylor's hand.

With only seconds left, Boston led 110-107. The Celtics knew what to do: Give the ball to the Cooz. And as he had done so often, he dribbled out the clock. The Celtics had won their fourth straight championship.

In thinking about his future, Cousy knew that he could become the coach of the Celtics, with Auerbach moving up to a front-office job. But Bob wanted no more of the grinding NBA schedule. "I've seen what Arnold goes through," he said. "No thanks."

Yet he could not bring himself to say good-bye to basketball. One day in the winter of 1962 there seemed to come a solution: Boston College officials asked Bob if he would take the job of coaching the BC basketball team.

Remembering how close he had once come to playing for Boston College, Cousy said that he would be delighted. But first he would have to consult with Walter Brown.

Brown did not take the news happily. The Celtics without Cousy? It would be like sending Jim Bowie into battle without a knife. Couldn't Bob play for just one more year?

Cousy could not refuse Brown, who had been kind and generous to him over the years. He went back to the Boston College officials; he told them he would have to turn down their offer.

But BC wanted him badly. OK, they said, here's what we will do: We will hold open the coaching job for a year. Cousy could play the entire 1962-63 season with the Celtics, then start coaching at BC in the fall of '63.

And so the news broke one afternoon: The Cooz would bow out as a player at the end of the 1962-63 NBA season. And in Boston town that day people talked about the skinny-looking guy in the Kelly green silks, with the big number 14 on his back. They talked about all the games he had won, the last-second baskets he had scored. Others talked about the New Breed of basketball players with one talent—a jump shot—and as they thought about Bob Cousy leaving basketball, they couldn't help but wonder whether they'd ever see a behind-the-back dribble again.

CHAPTER 14

A Prayer for a Last Favor

IN MANY ways, the 1962-63 season—his last—was the most important of them all for the Cooz. He made it clear right from the beginning that he wanted to go out a winner.

"You know," he told Phil Elderkin of the *Christian Science Monitor*, "it's very important to me—personally and financially—to go out on top. I want to quit, you might say, with the Cousy image intact. Ted Williams had the right idea. He quit baseball while he was ahead—while he could command the top dollar.

"But coming back this year has to be just a little bit of a gamble for me. Suppose I'm hurt or suppose I'd made a mistake—that I really couldn't do the job anymore?"

When the season started, Cousy seemed well able to do the job. "I'm more relaxed this year than I've ever been before," he said when asked about the way he bounced around the floor. "Other seasons I've tried to pace myself, to maybe hold just a little bit back. But there is no reason for that now. I go as hard as I can and let Auerbach decide when I've had enough.

"Still, mentally I'm fed up with the basketball grind —the traveling, the weird hours, the irregular eating. The games I enjoy. The other part—well, thirteen years is a long time."

As the season rolled toward the midpoint—the All-Star game—the grind was beginning to show its effects on Cousy's face. There were dark shadows under his eyes, and the long face seemed gaunt. He was pleasant with interviewers, though, even when they woke him from afternoon naps. "I suppose the explanation is that I know I won't have to be doing this much longer," he told *New Yorker* magazine writer Herbert Warren Wind.

"In a way, though, it was a good thing this trip [a coast-to-coast nightmare in which he had pulled a leg muscle] turned out to be so rough. The first couple of months this season, everything went so smoothly that I was wondering if I really wanted to retire. Well, I'm sure of it now. The schedule's just too brutal and the season's much too long.

"I see some youngster coming out to play me who's so fired up that the saliva is practically drooling from his mouth. I was probably like that myself when I was a kid and went out to play Bob Davies or Bob Wanzer or one of the other stars. Anyway, when I step out on the floor now, I have to key myself up consciously. I can't wait for it to come naturally anymore."

A few days later the tired Cousy went off to Los Angeles for what would be his 13th and final appearance in the NBA's East-West All-Star game. He had played in every All-Star game since its inception in 1951, but now he was thirty-five and an old man, and when people talked about this All-Star game, they talked about the West's great team—Elgin Baylor, Wilt Chamberlain (now playing with San Francisco) and Bob Pettit—a team that some said was the greatest ever assembled.

Early in the first period they were talking about the Cooz. Wheeling and dealing passes into Bill Russell, he led the underdog East into a 32-25 lead. And with Bill Russell scoring and rebounding, the East went on to win, 115-108. Wrote one reporter, Los Angeles' Bob Hunter: "Bob Cousy, the only man to play in all 13 All-Star games, made his farewell to the jeweled event a notable one, setting up the plays for the East in 25 minutes of sparkling work."

As the second half of the season began, the Celtics were well out in front in the East. And one of their big surprises was a rookie from Ohio State, John Havlicek. Someone asked Havlicek what it was like playing with Cousy.

"At first I couldn't believe he was real," said Havlicek, who'd been a second-team All-American. "I knew Cousy was good, but I never realized how good until I began to play with him.

"I was a cornerman in college, but Red Auerbach wanted me to play in the backcourt with the Celtics as well as in the corner. It meant I had to learn a new position, and without Bob's help I would never have been able to adjust so quickly.

"Cousy took me aside one day and told me I was overprotecting the ball—that if I didn't stop turning sideways to the man who was covering me, I'd never get a pass off.

"Bob told me to practice using my left hand as well as my right and to bring the ball up the floor facing my opponent. Otherwise I'd never be able to properly see the free man.

"He also told me I wasn't penetrating deeply enough into the other team's territory when I had the ball. He emphasized the importance of confidence."

Later Bob Brannum, who had played with Cousy and the Celtics early in the Fifties, told Phil Elderkin of the *Christian Science Monitor*: "I still visit Boston half a dozen times during the season to watch Bob, and he's just as effective as he ever was. When Cousy spots a loose ball, he knows it isn't going to jump into his hands just because his name is Bob Cousy. He knows he has to get down on the floor and fight for that ball just like the rawest rookie. . . . I'd say that Bob still has a couple of great years left."

Elderkin talked with Red Auerbach about Cousy. Red mentioned some obvious things: how this 6-foot-1 guy had competed sometimes head-to-head with 7-footers; how his great peripheral vision and photographic memory let him "see" every player on the court during a fast break; how his long arms made him such a great dribbler.

But then Auerbach talked about how Cousy had helped the Celtics in ways that never showed on a scoreboard. "When your star respects you," said Auerbach, "and will do anything you ask him to do, it immediately lessens your problems with other players. Rookies come in and right away they conform. They figure if Cousy lets Auerbach work him this hard, then who are they to complain?"

Later a morose Walter Brown was asked about the loss of Cousy. "I really don't want to talk about it," he said, the heartsickness showing in his voice. "I know I can't replace Cousy. How can you put a price on intangibles?"

The Celtics won the 1962-63 Eastern Division race in a breeze, finishing 10 games ahead of Syracuse. But in the opening game of the Eastern Division play-off with Cincinnati, the Celtics looked dreadfully tired, and the Royals won, 135-132.

"The Celtics are an old team," wrote one reporter, joining the majority who figured that Big O and his younger Royals would run right by the aging Celtics.

But the Celtic graybeards held on, and the two teams came down to a seventh game in the best-of-seven series. Of course, it was a familiar moment for the Celtics. "The Celtics," wrote a reporter, "*always* win the seventh game."

Perhaps not this year, said others, figuring that time had caught up with Boston. And they felt sorry for Cousy. If the Celtics lost this game to the Royals, he would be just another ex-basketball player going into retirement as the captain of a defeated team.

Cousy did not duck the pressure. He said publicly that "the prospect of going out a loser is unthinkable to me."

The day before the game, he began to feel the pressure "right here," he told *Sports Illustrated*'s John Underwood. He had not been able to eat the afternoon of the game. He had taken a pill to help him sleep the previous night. "People don't know what they're talking about," he said, "when they say the older you are the less you notice the tension. Each day you have to prove yourself all over again. Age doesn't count. I haven't spoken to my wife on a game day in twelve years."

In the dressing room he barely grunted at the other players, drifting off into that fog-enwrapped world. He trotted out onto the court at the Boston Garden—perhaps for the last time—with that same preoccupied frown on his face, the glaze over the eyes.

But when the game began, he was a whirling fury, pulling lightning out of a bottle as he spearheaded one fast break after another. In one span, he scored four of Boston's five baskets. He threw three quick passes to Sam Jones for another six points. The Royals looked bewildered as the Celtics coasted home to win the Eastern title, 142-131.

The Celtics shouted and laughed in their dressing room, the photographers' flashbulbs throwing glints of light against the bare walls. They photographed

Cousy, his black hair matted with sweat, and Auerbach and Russell and Sam Jones. There was a sense of final victory among the Celtics, even though they still had to face Elgin Baylor and the Lakers in a best-of-seven series. You felt now that the Cooz was going to go out a winner.

And he did. He would come limping back onto the court at Los Angeles, his sprained ankle taped, and he would pick up the Celtics and carry them to an unprecedented fifth straight NBA championship. He would dribble out the clock in center court, and when the final buzzer ripsawed through the bedlam of noise, he'd throw the ball high into the air, and his lips would move in a prayer, a prayer of thanksgiving that God had allowed him to leave a winner.

CHAPTER 15

Joe Dillon Said It Best

IT WAS Sunday, March 17, 1963—St. Patrick's Day—and the streets of Boston were jammed with men and women showing the green. Thousands of them made their way slowly toward the Boston Garden, where signs proclaimed that this was "Bob Cousy Day." Since 1946 this kid from New York had been thrilling Boston, and now Boston was on its way to the Garden to let him know what it thought of him.

The Celtics were playing the Syracuse Nats this afternoon. In the month ahead would come the exciting play-off battles with the Royals and Lakers, battles that would bring to Boston a fifth NBA championship. But as the big crowd looked down on the brightly lit court at the Boston Garden this afternoon, there was talk only of the Cooz.

The crowd bought souvenir programs, tinted green, titled BOB COUSY DAY. In the center spread a letter was reproduced. "It is a pleasure," said the letter, "for me to join with the sports world in this tribute to you," and it was signed John F. Kennedy.

The day had begun for Cousy when he arrived from Syracuse at two in the morning on a storm-tossed plane. He had checked in at a hotel, slept fitfully, rising finally after four hours in bed and going to Mass.

On the way to the Garden, he looked out at the leaden sky and told a reporter: "I hope my mother and father can get a plane into Boston from New York. I wouldn't want them to miss this."

He posed for photographers in the Celtics' dressing room, and told reporters that he had written a speech. He laughed, nervously. "I hope people understand why I had to write it out. Otherwise I don't think I'd be able to go through with it. I even broke down writing the darned speech."

Red Auerbach came in. He had been scouting some college players the previous night, so Cousy had coached the Celtics in their game at Syracuse. "I told them to win it for you, Arnold," said Cousy, grinning. "Were they inspired! They want me to stay here and you to go coach at BC."

The players roared, the laughs led by the shattering *ack-ack-ack-ack* of Bill Russell. Auerbach flushed and laughed; there was a wet glint in his eyes.

A policeman stuck his head into the room and looked at Cousy. "Time," he said.

Cousy picked up a basketball as he had done so

often in the past. But this day was different. "I hope I do okay," he said to no one in particular.

He led the file of players out onto the court, and a thunderclap of sound shook the Garden as the crowd saw the black-haired guy wearing number 14 come dribbling the ball onto the court. Someone had brought Juliet Cousy to the side of the court, and Bob stopped and kissed his mother.

Ringing the court were people out of the Cousy past who had come from far places to honor him this day: his mother and father, Easy Ed Macauley and Doggie Julian, and over on the Syracuse bench, grinning Dolph Schayes.

Cousy played against Schayes and Syracuse as he played every game—all out. In the third period, he threw in a little scoop shot, his 1,000th point of the season, the fifth year in a row that he had scored more than 1,000 points. With two minutes to go in the fourth period and the Celtics on their way to an easy 125-116 triumph, Auerbach got up from the bench. He signaled to K. C. Jones, who ran to the scorers' table, said something, then ran onto the court when time was called.

Cousy turned and ran off, and the crowd was on its feet, 13,909 yelling people. And they kept on yelling and cheering, their roaring sweeping over the court, on and on, and finally a referee blew a whistle and the game began again. The Celtics scored four more points and Syracuse six, but that din never once subsided, the cheers swelling over Cousy's head as he sat on the bench, his head bowed.

But now it was a half hour earlier, at half time of the Syracuse-Boston game, and the Cousy Day ceremonies were about to begin. The TV cameras pointed toward center court, where Cousy stood in his white warm-up suit, Mary Patricia on his left, Missie on his right, and Marie Colette next to her.

Red Auerbach walked out to where Cousy was standing and read the letter from President Kennedy. Then Auerbach looked up at the crowd and said, "You people are sorry to see Cousy go? How do you think I feel?" The crowd yelled and Cousy and Auerbach hugged each other.

Walter Brown came out to present Cousy with a Cadillac, a gift of the fans, and then the big blunt Irishman looked over at Bob and said, "And I'm the guy who didn't want Cousy. . . . Some genius, huh?" And again the crowd laughed and applauded.

There were more gifts. A little blond girl, twelve-year-old Martha O'Grady, gave Mass missals to Cousy's two daughters. Martha had posed with Bob for posters to raise funds for the fight against cystic fibrosis, a killer of children. Little Martha looked at Cousy, and suddenly the Cooz was leaning down and Martha had both arms entwined around his neck.

There were more gifts and you could see that the two little Cousy girls were starting to cry, but Missie— her lower lip trembling—stayed dry-eyed. Later she explained that "I cried so much yesterday [when the Celtic wives gave her a luncheon] that there was nothing left."

Then, out at center court, the announcer began to introduce Cousy, but he didn't have to, as the crowd began to roar a tribute. Up in the press box, crusty reporters were on their feet, applauding. Cousy held up his hands, but the roaring went on—one minute, two minutes, three minutes—and then it died down a little and he began to speak:

"Ladies and gentleman, I hope you'll allow me to use some prepared notes that I made this afternoon," he said, the *r*'s still sometimes coming out as *l*'s. "Normally I think this doesn't fit the occasion and that perhaps it lacks a little sincerity and warmth. However, there are so many important things that I would like to say that I want to make sure that it gets done.

"You know in thirteen years since I left Holy Cross, I've had the occasion to stand many times in front of an audience but I'm afraid that the task has never been quite as difficult as it is today. It seems it's difficult to find mere words that seem so inadequate to say the things . . ."

He began to sob, and little Marie handed him her handkerchief, though tears were streaming down her face, too.

The crowd began to yell, encouraging words, as Cousy bowed his head to hide the tears, and then the roaring got louder and for 15 seconds the people were yelling and cheering.

The Cooz began to speak again, and then stopped, sobbing, and said: "I hope you will bear with me for just a few moments."

He began again: "To start, I would like to thank the editors throughout the country for their generous recognition. I think of the awards I have been fortunate enough to receive . . ."

His voice stopped on a sob, but somehow he kept going: ". . . none mean quite as much as this one. In thanking the Syracuse Nationals for their gift, I would like to say that it has been an honor and a privilege for me to compete against their teams. Throughout the years they have always personified the type of hustling . . ."

He broke down for a few seconds, then continued: ". . . determined ball club that I admire most." The crowd began to applaud, and he stopped, trying to regain his composure.

"On behalf of my daughters," he went on, "who thank God as you can see resemble their mother, I would like to thank the Cystic Fibrosis Foundation. You have heard me on many occasions appeal to you for help in combating this dreadful children's disease . . ."

He was sobbing again.

". . . and you have always responded magnificently."

He went on to give his thanks for other gifts, including ones from the Governor of Massachusetts and the Mayor of Boston. "In this regard," he said, "I can only say that if I had to do it over again . . ."

Now he was crying openly.

". . . I just couldn't imagine playing anywhere but Boston."

Applause rang through the Garden for 10 seconds.

After thanking the Celtic players and their wives and the Boston press, he said: "I have been asked many times this year what I will miss most about no longer playing. This is the easiest question I have ever had to respond to.

"The things that I feel in leaving Red, Buddy LeRoux, and my teammates cannot be recorded on paper nor expressed in words . . ."

He began to sob and the applause swelled for 15 seconds.

"At least I don't have the ability to do so. I will say simply that the deepest regret I have in leaving is no longer being able to share the camaraderie and *esprit de corps* and the common bond of competition and the inspiration I have received being captain of this team.

"I would feel as if we had never won a ball game. I would feel as if we had been bank clerks together, circus performers, or any occupation on the face of this earth, just as long as we could have participated together. . . ."

Tears were coming down his cheeks, and he put Marie's handkerchief to his face.

"Lastly, ladies and gentlemen, I would like to thank you wonderful, wonderful fans of New England that have given the Celtics and myself such continued sincere support. You have been so helpful . . ."

The words were coming out between sobs.

". . . and contributed to our success in so many ways. You have written me congratulation when we've been successful. You have written letters of encouragement when I've been depressed or in a slump. I only hope that my playing has in a small way served to repay you for your many kindnesses."

Applause burst from the balconies, sweeping down around the skinny figure at the mike. Yes, this crowd was telling the Cooz, it had been repaid in full.

"An affair like this," said Cousy, not trying to stop the tears any longer, "takes only a few minutes to transpire. But please be assured that it will leave my family and me with a memory that will warm us throughout our lives.

"Finally I would like you all to join with me in appreciation to my mother and father, Missie and my daughters, for the wonderful inspiration they have given me throughout the years.

"Thank you and may God bless you all."

He stepped back from the mike, his head down, the girls crying beside him, his wife with a stricken look on her face, and the crowd roared down its feelings—for 30 seconds, a minute, two minutes, three minutes, and by actual count made later on the television tape, three minutes and 20 seconds. It stopped only when Cousy put his arms around his family and walked to the sideline.

Up high in the balconies, grown men couldn't look into each other's eyes because tears welled there. But on that day, no one better expressed how Boston and the world of sports felt about Bob Cousy than a leather-lunged fan named Joe Dillon.

At one of the moments in Cousy's speech when he began to sob, there was a sudden silence in the Garden. And then Joe Dillon, a maintenance worker by trade, yelled. It was short and it wasn't poetic, but it came from this crowd's heart as Joe Dillon told it all to Bob Cousy:

"We love ya, Cooz!"

Bob Cousy's All-Time Records

At Andrew Jackson High School

	Games	FG	FT	Pts.	Avg.
1944-45	10	37	15	89	8.9
1945-46	18	134	51	319	17.7

At Holy Cross

	Games	FG	FT	Pts.	Avg.
1946-47	30	91	45	227	7.5
1947-48	30	207	72	486	16.2
1948-49	27	195	90	480	17.7
1949-50	30	216	150	582	19.4

NBA Regular Season

Year	Team	Games	FG	FT	Reb.	Ass'ts	PF	Pts.	Avg.
1950-51	Bos.	69	401	276	474	341	185	1078	15.6
1951-52	Bos.	66	512	409	421	441	190	1433	21.7
1952-53	Bos.	71	464	479	449	547	227	1407	19.8
1953-54	Bos.	72	486	411	394	518	201	1383	19.2
1954-55	Bos.	71	522	460	424	557	165	1504	21.2
1955-56	Bos.	72	440	476	492	642	206	1356	18.8
1956-57	Bos.	64	478	363	309	478	134	1319	20.6
1957-58	Bos.	65	445	277	322	463	136	1167	18.0
1958-59	Bos.	65	484	329	359	557	135	1297	20.0
1959-60	Bos.	75	568	319	352	715	146	1455	19.4
1960-61	Bos.	76	513	352	331	591	196	1378	18.1
1961-62	Bos.	75	462	251	261	584	135	1175	15.7
1962-63	Bos.	76	392	298	201	515	175	1003	13.2
	Career	917	6167	4700	4789	6949	2231	16,955	18.5

NBA Play-offs

Year	Team	Games	FG	FT	Reb.	Ass'ts	PF	Pts.	Avg.
1950-51	Bos.	2	9	10	15	12	8	28	14.0
1951-52	Bos.	3	26	41	12	19	13	93	31.0
1952-53	Bos.	6	46	61	25	37	21	153	25.5
1953-54	Bos.	6	33	60	32	38	20	126	21.0
1954-55	Bos.	7	53	46	43	65	26	152	21.7
1955-56	Bos.	3	28	23	24	26	4	79	26.3
1956-57	Bos.	10	67	68	61	93	27	202	20.2
1957-58	Bos.	11	67	64	71	82	20	198	18.0
1958-59	Bos.	11	72	70	76	119	28	214	19.5
1959-60	Bos.	13	80	39	48	116	27	199	15.3
1960-61	Bos.	10	50	67	43	91	33	167	16.7
1961-62	Bos.	14	86	52	64	123	43	224	16.0
1962-63	Bos.	13	72	39	32	116	44	183	14.1
Career		109	689	640	546	837	314	2018	19.4

NBA All-Star Games

Year	Team	Min.	FG	FT	Reb.	Ass'ts	PF	Pts.
1951	Bos.	—	2	4	9	8	3	8
1952	Bos.	33	4	1	4	13	3	9
1953	Bos.	36	4	7	5	3	1	15
1954	Bos.	34	6	8	11	4	1	20
1955	Bos.	35	7	6	9	5	1	20
1956	Bos.	24	2	3	7	2	6	7
1957	Bos.	28	4	2	5	7	0	10
1958	Bos.	31	8	4	5	10	0	20
1959	Bos.	32	4	5	5	4	0	13
1960	Bos.	26	1	0	5	8	2	2
1961	Bos.	33	2	0	3	8	6	4
1962	Bos.	31	4	3	6	8	2	11
1963	Bos.	25	4	0	4	6	2	8
TOTAL		368	52	43	78	86	27	147

Index

Anderson, Dave, 19
Andrew Jackson Community Center, 61
Andrew Jackson High School, 51, 52, 55, 56, 67-70, 72, 86, 112, 136
Arizin, Paul, 101
Arkin, Morty, 53, 54, 56, 57, 62
Auerbach, Arnold "Red," 9, 12, 13, 15, 22, 23, 31, 97, 99-103, 105, 107-11, 115-18, 123, 124, 134, 139, 141-43, 149, 150, 155, 169, 170, 174-76, 178, 180-82, 185, 186

Barnett, Dick, 14, 25, 26
Barrett, Ernie, 141
Basketball Is My Life, 34, 43, 47, 50, 61, 84, 85, 124
Baylor, Elgin, 11-13, 156, 163, 169, 174, 178
Birch, Paul, 103
Bobb, Nelson, 102
"Bob Cousy Day," 179-87
Bollinger, Charlie, 74, 76
Boryla, Vince, 149
Boston Celtics, 9, 10, 12-15, 20, 21, 23, 28, 30-32, 84, 85, 91, 96-99, 101, 103-07, 109-11, 115-18, 125, 127, 128, 131, 135-40, 142-47, 149, 150, 156, 157, 159, 160, 165, 166, 168-70, 174-76, 178-81, 185
 five straight championships, 10, 178, 179, 181
 vs Cincinnati Royals, 141, 142
 vs New York Knickerbockers, 159, 160
 vs Philadelphia Warriors, 101-03
 vs St. Louis Hawks, 118, 119
Boston College, 70-73, 76, 170

Boston Garden, 18, 23, 24, 26, 30, 32, 74, 76, 78, 80, 82, 92, 101, 105, 107, 115, 126, 150, 155, 156, 163, 177, 179-81
Brannum, Bob, 175
Braun, Carl, 29
Brown, Walter, 21, 95-98, 107-10, 116, 117, 124, 128, 168, 170, 176, 182

Catholic Youth League, 60
Chamberlain, Wilt "the Stilt," 163
Chicago Stags, 97, 98
Cincinnati Royals, 139, 158, 164, 176
 vs Boston Celtics, 141, 142
Clifton, Sweetwater, 28, 29
Coleman, Jack, 119
Conley, Gene, 166
Cooper, Chuck, 21, 22, 101
Costello, Larry, 31
Cousy, Joseph, 34-37, 44-49, 51, 73, 181
Cousy, Juliet, 34-37, 42-49, 51, 54, 60, 73, 181
Cousy, Marie Colette, 125, 134, 135, 182, 183
Cousy, Mary Patricia, 125, 134, 135, 182
Cousy, Robert Joseph (Bob), "the Cooz"
 as a boy, 33-56
 learns to play basketball, 52-55
 in high school, 56-69, 86
 plays on junior varsity team, 56, 57, 61, 62
 plays on varsity team, 56, 60, 63, 66-69
 in college, 18, 19, 26, 27, 71-97
 as professional, 9-16, 19-32, 96-126, 129, 130, 135, 136, 138-87

"Houdini of the Hardwood," 54, 130
  as businessman, 129-32, 134, 167
Cousy, Mrs. Robert Joseph (*see also* Ritterbusch, Marie "Missie"), 96, 126, 127, 129, 131-33, 135, 166, 182, 183
Curran, Bob, 74

Davies, Bob, 27, 113, 173
Devlin, Father John, 79
Dillon, Joe, 187

Eisenhower, Dwight D., 133

Faust, Larry, 113
Field, Wes, 52, 53, 55-57
Fort Wayne Pistons, 103, 115
Fulks, Joe, 101

Gallatin, Harry "the Horse," 112
Gelman, Steve, 113
Goodman, Irv, 140, 148
Gottlieb, Eddie, 98, 99, 102
Graham, Otto, 75
Grummond, Lew, 52, 55-57, 60-63, 65-67
Guarila, Gene, 166

Hagan, Cliff, 116, 119, 150
Haggerty, Ken, 72, 74
Hanson, Vic, 68-70
Haran, Father Pat, 132
Harlem Globetrotters, 28, 29, 116
Harney, Charles, 21
Havlicek, John, 10, 174, 175
Heinsohn, Tommy (the Gunner), 10, 13-15, 30, 117, 118, 125, 127, 134, 138, 142, 143, 147, 155, 166
Higgins, Frank, 58-60, 67, 70, 71
Hirshberg, Al, 34, 124, 143, 144
Holy Cross, 18, 19, 26, 71-87, 89-97, 100, 129, 132, 137
  Crusaders, 76-78, 82, 87, 90, 92-94
  vs Loyola, 18, 19, 26, 80-84, 90, 92
Hornung, Paul, 19, 20

Irish, Ned, 98, 99

Johnston, Neil, 24, 25, 105, 112, 148-50
Jones, K. C., 10, 21, 166, 181
Jones, Sam, 10, 147, 166, 178
Julian, Alvin "Doggie," 72-74, 76-85, 90, 97, 181

Kaftan, George, 74, 77, 90-92, 94, 100
Kennedy, Angus, 51-53, 55-57, 59-61
Kennedy, John F., 180, 182
Kilduff, Joan, 60, 73, 85, 86

LaRusso, Rudy, 14
Laska, Andy, 27, 76, 77
Laurelton team, 60, 61
LeRoux, Buddy, 9, 10, 12, 31, 185
Long Island Press League, 60
Los Angeles Lakers, 10-15, 25, 169, 178
Los Angeles Sports Arena, 9, 11
Loscutoff, "Jungle Jim," 117, 118, 149, 166
Loyola, 18, 19, 26, 78, 81
  vs Holy Cross, 18, 19, 26, 80-84, 90, 92

Macauley, Easy Ed, 23, 101, 108, 112, 115, 116, 118, 119, 150, 181
Madison Square Garden, 27-29, 67, 68, 111-14, 125, 159, 161
Martin, Slater "Dugie," 70, 113, 119, 161
McClellan, Al, 70-72
McGuire, Dick, 112
McKinney, Bones, 100, 103, 104
McNeill, Bobby, 159
Mikan, George, 105, 112, 163
Minneapolis Lakers, 105, 115, 156, 157, 168
Mogus, Leo, 102, 103
Mullaney, Dave, 74
Mullaney, Joe, 26, 74, 75, 100

Nagel, Gerry, 18, 19
National Basketball Association, 11, 14, 17, 21, 96-99, 102-04, 116
  All-Star games, 24, 25, 27, 28, 112-14, 159, 174
  determining champion of, 104

player's union, 128, 129
playoff and championship games, 10-15, 30-32, 104-08, 115, 119-23, 150-57, 165, 166, 168, 169, 176, 177
NCAA, 77, 84, 89, 94
New York City All-High School team, 69, 74
New York Knickerbockers, 28, 98, 99, 107, 115, 146, 155, 156, 159
vs Boston Celtics, 159, 160
Nichols, Jack, 116, 147

O'Connell, Dermie, 26, 74, 100
O'Connell Playground, 47, 49, 51-53, 55, 59, 60
Oesting, Ray, 93
Oftring, Frank, 76, 87, 88, 91-93, 129

"Persecution of Minority Groups," 89
Pettit, Bob, 24, 119, 150
Philadelphia Warriors, 98, 99, 104, 105, 107, 115, 145, 146, 150, 165, 166, 168
vs Boston Celtics, 101-03
Phillip, Andy, 98, 99, 116, 147
Podoloff, Maurice, 98, 128
Pollard, Jim, 113
Public School Athletic League, Queens division of, 67, 68

Ramsey, Frank, 10, 31, 117, 138, 147, 166
Risen, Arnie, 116, 117, 147
Ritterbusch, Ed, 86
Ritterbusch, Marie "Missie" (Mrs. Bob Cousy), 86-89
Robertson, Oscar, 70, 158-61, 163-65
Ross, Ben, 23-25

Russell, Bill, 10, 12, 15, 16, 21, 30, 116-18, 147, 155, 163, 166, 178

Sailors, Kenny, 75
St. Albans Lindens Juniors, 59-61
St. Louis Hawks, 118, 119, 143, 150, 156, 157, 161, 165
vs Boston Celtics, 118, 119
St. Pascal's parish team, 60, 61
Sanders, Tom (Satch), 10, 166
Schayes, Dolph, 24, 30, 112, 128, 156, 181
Schmidt, Mike, 86
Sears, Kenny, 149
Senesky, George, 101
Share, Charlie, 97
Sharman, Bill (Willie), 105, 108, 112, 116, 118, 119, 140, 144, 145, 147, 155, 165
Sharry, Joe, 127-31
Sheary, Buster, 90
Spahn, Warren, 74
Stassen, Harold, 133
Syracuse Nationals, 30-32, 105-08, 115, 125, 145, 146, 156, 166, 176, 179, 181, 184

Tri-Cities, 96-99
Tsioropoulos, Lou, 147

Wanzer, Bobby, 113, 173
West, Jerry, 11, 14, 163, 169
White House, 133
Wind, Herbert Warren, 18, 173
Worcester, Mass., 17, 20, 27, 29, 72-74, 77-79, 87, 88, 95-97, 107, 108, 110, 125, 127, 132, 166

Yardley, George, 24

Zaslofsky, Max, 98, 99

The Author

JOHN DEVANEY has been writing sports stories for the past fifteen years, as editor of *Parade* magazine and as a contributor to *Sport, Saturday Evening Post, P.geant, Catholic Digest,* and the Fawcett annual sport magazines. He has known Bob Cousy for the past ten years, has visited his summer camp for boys at Graylag, New Hampshire, and has done a number of magazine articles on the great basketball star. Mr. Devaney, who lives in New York City, is currently at work on a basketball instructional book.